A Tour of
British Bird Reserves

A Tour of
British Bird Reserves

Valerie Russell

The Crowood Press

First published in 1986 by
THE CROWOOD PRESS
Crowood House,
Ramsbury, Marlborough,
Wiltshire SN8 2HE

British Library Cataloguing in Publication Data

Russell, Valerie
    A tour of British reserves.
    1. Bird reserves – Great Britain
    I. Title
    639.9'782941   QL676.5

    ISBN 0-946284-03-2

Dedication

M. Without whom it would not have been such fun.

Picture credits

Black and white photos

Barry Lillycrapp: *pages* 11, 13, 20, 33, 35, 45, 49, 54, 65, 76, 85, 88, 93, 99, 119,
    135, 137, 147, 152, 155, 161.
Michael Edwards: *pages* 17, 25, 59, 68, 74, 83, 97, 102, 105, 123, 125, 129, 133,
    145, 149, 163, 167.
Will Bown: *pages* 19, 39, 42, 113, 127, 141.
Valerie Russell: *pages* 22, 27, 30, 51, 61, 80, 112, 115.
Martin Smith: *page* 71.

Colour photos

Michael Edwards: *plate* 15
Paul Kirby: *plates* 5, 19
Paul Kirby and David Moss-Allison: *plate* 10
Barry Lillycrapp: *plates* 2, 4, 6, 8, 9, 12, 13, 17, 21, 24, 27
David Moss-Allison: *plates* 16, 25
Valerie Russell: *plates* 1, 3, 7, 11, 14, 18, 20, 22, 23, 26, 29, 30, 31, 33
Swift Picture Library: *plates* 28, 32

Typeset by Eagle Graphics (Phototypesetting) Limited, Ilkley, W. Yorkshire
Printed in Great Britain

Contents

Introduction

Choosing the reserves to visit for the purposes of this book was very difficult indeed. There are, after all, well over 3,000 nature reserves in Britain, and on so many of them the bird-life is rich and varied. I therefore made what is essentially a very personal choice of reserves where the nature-lover with a special interest in birds may expect to see appreciable numbers of birds without undue difficulty. With this in mind, I visited reserves – not all bird reserves as such – that are reasonably accessible and which, with a few exceptions, do not require permits. A number of striking reserves which are situated on islands have, therefore, not been included because access to these is often quite difficult.

The reserves chosen belong to or are administered by a variety of bodies, including the Royal Society for the Protection of Birds, the Nature Conservancy Council, and local Naturalists' Trusts. In the case of the latter, membership of the reader's local trust nearly always gains entry to reserves belonging to other county trusts. Most naturalists with an interest in birds will probably already belong to the RSPB, but for those who do not, entry to its reserves is, where applicable, gained by payment of a fee.

Geographically, the reserves are reasonably widely distributed throughout Britain, but as the most spectacular numbers of birds are so often seen around the coast, there is a predominance of reserves in those areas. This is reflected in the book.

My overall aim is to cover as many aspects of the reserves as possible; consequently I have mentioned, albeit briefly, the general wildlife of the reserves as well as the birds. I hope that this approach will appeal to the reader who, like myself, has a wide-ranging interest in natural history, rather than specialist knowledge.

I hope, too, that the book will help the reader to obtain as much pleasure and interest from the reserves as we did. It will be a bonus if it also draws attention to the really vital work being done by the various conservation bodies in establishing and maintaining these reserves, which are so important to the wildlife of Britain.

South-east England

Rye Harbour
Local Nature Reserve

Managing body   East Sussex County Council.
Access   TQ 9419. Rye Harbour.
Other information   Information centre in car-park. Leaflets. Nature trail.

Although they may appear featureless and unexciting to the casual observer, the expanses of shingle ridges interspersed with disused gravel pits that are the most important characteristics of the Rye Harbour Local Nature Reserve and SSSI (Site of Special Scientific Interest) in Sussex will, none the less, bring a gleam to the eye of any naturalist – especially the birdwatcher and the botanist. Just a brief inspection of the attractive information centre in the Rye Harbour car-park, with its illuminated displays of colour slides and texts describing the flora and fauna of the reserve, reinforced our initial impression that this was a place to be savoured.

Our visit was in mid-May, but Rye Harbour is a place where, for the birdwatcher at least, the time of year is immaterial. In winter, wildfowl and waders can be seen off shore, along the shore, and around the gravel pits; in spring and autumn the variety of birds is enormous, as the harbour is a cross-roads of migration routes; while in summer the nesting species include the little tern – the story of whose survival and revival on this reserve is a truly heartening one.

Before setting off to explore the reserve, we obtained from the warden's house (the phone number is in the information centre) two pamphlets. The first gave details of things to be seen and a map of the 1,792 acre reserve, and the second a description of the three-quarter mile guided walk along the north-eastern boundary beside the River Rother. Also available, and well worth reading, is a report by R.C. Knight and P.C. Haddon (former warden and assistant) entitled Little Terns in England and Wales (1977-79), which describes the conservation work undertaken at Rye in the successful efforts to encourage little terns to re-establish themselves in greater numbers on the reserve.

Armed with the two pamphlets, we set off on the guided walk, which took us down a private road on the western bank of the river. A short distance along on the left is a small area of tidal salt marsh, where redshanks (one of the reserve's breeding species) were feeding, probably on the shrimp-like *Corophium volutator* which lives in U-shaped tubes in the substrate between the sea purslane and spartina grass. On the opposite side of the road is arable land reclaimed from salt marsh, and here we saw a number of meadow pipits and heard, but did not see, reed buntings in the herbage in the drainage dyke. In winter, rock pipits frequent this area.

A little further on, still on the right, where the arable begins to give way to shingle, we heard and saw one of the ringed plovers which are such a feature of the Rye Harbour reserve. This one, like many we saw subsequently, was engaged in diversionary behaviour – flying in front of us, landing on the tarmac or shingle and running along in front – although on this and other occasions they did not employ their typical tactic of feigning a damaged wing to entice us away from their nest sites.

We followed the walk down to the mouth of the river and the shore. There we saw some of the herring and black-backed gulls that roost and breed on the reserve. We also saw one or two of the little and common terns – the little terns easily distinguishable by their small size, yellow bills with black tips and white forehead, compared with the larger size and the black-tipped crimson bills of the common terns.

At various times of the year, an exciting variety of birds has been recorded around the mouth of the river. The 1982 Annual Report of the Management Committee tells of an exceptional number of red-throated divers in the bay during January, amounting to about 100 birds, some 28 great crested grebes, and about 1,200 guillemots on passage. Eiders, scoters, mergansers, smews, and Mediterranean gulls are just some of the birds that have been seen at various times.

Although the guided walk ends at the shore, there is a great deal more of the reserve open to the public. Retracing our steps, we turned left onto the road behind the shingle storm ridge and made our way – with considerable difficulty – towards the gravel pit known as Ternery Pool, about three-quarters of a mile distant. The difficulty was occasioned by a really vicious south-westerly gale and driving rain which made walking a battle for each step and the use of binoculars a virtual impossibility!

It was, however, still possible to see the various shingle plants and the shingle itself which, with the birds, are the most important features of the reserve. The shingle ridges are of more than usual interest because they have been built up as the result of storms over many hundreds of years. Fortunately, the major storms were recorded, so the ages of the present ridges are known. From this it has been possible to date, with some accuracy, the stages in succession of the vegetation from the bare shingle of the storm crest to the stable grasslands further inland.

Among the 300 or so species of plants recorded on the reserve, those which show adaptations to an exposed maritime way of life are, perhaps, the most interesting. One such adaptation is seen in the coastal form of curled dock, in which the fruits, unlike those of the inland variety, are able to float in salt water. Others, such as the yellow wall pepper and the maritime form of herb Robert, adopt a low-growing form. When we were there, the comparatively uncommon sea pea was just coming into flower, as was the seakale. Other typical maritime plants to be seen at the appropriate times include yellow horned poppy, sea rocket and the scentless mayweed. A British rarity found at Rye is the least lettuce, a member of the daisy (Compositae) family.

As we struggled along the road, we saw an increasing number of common and little terns. Visitors to Rye Harbour are asked to keep to the recognised roads and paths; this is particularly important in the nesting season, as the nests of breeding species such as the oystercatcher, ringed plover and little tern are no more than scrapes in the sand or shingle. This, together with the cryptic colour of the eggs, makes them liable to destruction by unwary human feet.

A proportion of the reserve is guarded by wire-strand fencing with notices requesting that visitors do not trespass on the enclosed areas. It is this fencing which has played such an important part in the revival of the little terns by discouraging human disturbance and predation by foxes.

The factual, yet none the less enthralling, account of how the wardens and their volunteer helpers have, since 1976, striven to halt and then reverse the decline in the breeding colony of little terns is contained in the report mentioned at the beginning of this chapter. The colony, the last of twelve that existed between Hythe and Hastings until the 1960s, had been reduced from about eighty pairs in 1946 to just two in 1974. Initial protective measures at Rye included the erection of single-strand wire fencing around the main nesting areas prior to the nesting season, with notice boards requesting people not to enter the enclosures. This was reinforced by wardens patrolling between eight and fifteen hours a day. However, of the sixteen pairs that made nesting attempts, only two were successful, and there was also a big fall in success among the other ground nesting species – ringed plovers, lapwings and oystercatchers.

The nesting species include the little tern, the story of whose survival and revival on this reserve is a truly heartening one.

Predation by either foxes or badgers during darkness was suspected and, as a deterrent to the former, an area of ten metres square around a single nest was enclosed with electric fencing. From this nest, which was in the middle of an area where nine other nesting attempts had failed, two young hatched but, sadly, wandered away and disappeared after five days. The indications were, however, that a large mammal was responsible for the general failure, and it was decided that the next year a larger area would be enclosed with electric fencing, and night-time patrols undertaken during the breeding season.

In 1978, the single-strand and non-electrified fencing was extended to include other suitable nesting areas, and the three-strand electric wiring enclosed three hectares of the most favoured areas. But these 'best laid schemes' did not take into account the perversity of the birds and all but four pairs nested in an entirely new site some distance away to the west. Of the fourteen pairs, only three young were reared.

It was conclusively established by night-time observations that foxes were the principal predators; it was also shown that the electric fencing was ineffective against them due to the high insulative properties of the shingle which protected them against shocks except in very wet conditions. It was concluded that the 'success' within the small electrically fenced area the previous year was not due to the electrification, but merely to the fact that it was a small barrier.

Nothing daunted, plans were made for the following year to re-fence the area, plus some additional ground, with a much improved nine-strand structure incorporating both live and earthed wires. Swift action had to be taken when the first ten pairs of terns showed signs of nesting west of the enclosure, and twenty-two plastic flags were placed to discourage them. Although some eggs were laid in the 'wrong' place, most pairs took the hint and nested within the enclosed zone. Twenty-eight nesting attempts resulted in thirteen chicks being reared to the flying stage. More significantly, not one egg or chick was lost to foxes within that zone.

As one predator was deterred, another – a kestrel – was believed to have taken about twenty-eight chicks within the course of a month. In the small colonies of little terns that exist at Rye and other places, this constitutes a very serious threat, as any form of control of kestrels (a protected species) is illegal. However, the protective measures to reduce human and fox disturbance have been successful, and in 1980 (the latest figures available at the time of writing), the most successful year so far, forty-three pairs made fifty-one nesting attempts, with fifty-eight young reared to flying stage.

Apart from the sheer delight for birdwatchers of seeing these, the smallest of the European terns, the importance of the work being done at Rye to encourage one of Britain's rarest breeding sea-birds cannot be overestimated. A survey in 1980 showed 2,000 pairs throughout Britain, and Rye has once again become a major British colony, thanks to the dedication of its wardens, its Management Committee, and the band of 100 or more volunteer wardens who guard the site throughout the nesting season.

We certainly enjoyed seeing the terns, and as we approached the path to the Ternery Pool with its two hides, the number flying overhead increased, and we saw not only the common and little species, but also a number of Sandwich terns. The hides (which are open to the public) are approached by sunken pathways and, as always, we felt a tingle of excitement as we entered them and raised the flaps. I think that when a birdwatcher no longer has that wonderful feeling of anticipation when entering a hide, it must be time to give up!

At Rye Harbour, a yellow wagtail was flitting round the Ternery Pool margin to one side of the hide.

The Ternery Pool is quite an expanse of water, dotted with several islands which are managed for the nesting common terns and also, since 1980, for sand martins. A number of common terns were already in residence, occupying their usual sites on the most westerly of the islands, which they favour. Although we did not see the males presenting the females with fish in the usual courtship ceremony on this occasion, we did watch, with some amusement, the very aggressive defence of territory against an intruding coot. Shrieking harshly, the terns dive-bombed the coot repeatedly, the coot retaliating by making determined upward stabs with its bill as the terns swooped down on it. Eventually, finding itself out-numbered, it retreated into the reeds and out of danger.

At the far side of the pool from the south shore hide there was a noisy collection of black-headed gulls and a few herring gulls, all of which nest there, and also a number of little grebes and tufted ducks. A small party of knots arrived, staying on one of the islands

13

for a short time, and we were lucky to see a black-tailed godwit – a relatively rare visitor to the reserve, although the bar-tailed species is usually seen in small numbers later in the year. A yellow wagtail was flitting round the pool margin to one side of the hide, and a number of wheatears were also present, some of which would, hopefully, nest in the boxes provided on the reserve.

Moving round to the hide on the eastern shore of the pool, we had good views of the island on which artificial nesting banks with sand-charged plastic pipes have been built. These are used successfully by small numbers of sand martins each year.

The Ternery Pool is certainly one of the focal points of the reserve both as a breeding and as a wintering centre. The fringe vegetation, such as reeds, sea-club rush and glaucous bulrush together with the horned and fennel-leaved pondweed in the water itself, provides food for the birds in the form of seeds and is also shelter for nests. The nesting birds include little grebes, tufted ducks, shelducks, reed warblers and reed buntings, in addition to the gulls and terns already mentioned.

The main excitement during our visit was the little terns, but the list of species which may be seen at other times of the year makes Rye Harbour a place to return to again and again. Briefly, over twenty-six species of small waders have been recorded there either on passage or wintering, including avocets, whimbrels, greenshanks, sanderlings, little stints and spotted redshanks. The fourteen or more species of gulls and terns include the black tern and little gull, while, among birds of prey, marsh and hen harriers, hobbies and even the very occasional sighting of an osprey and a red kite have been recorded. Smaller birds include at least ten species of warblers, snow buntings and an occasional alpine swift, while the owl family is represented by little, short-eared and long-eared. Wildfowl are plentiful, particularly in winter. White-fronted, greylag, Canada, barnacle and brent geese have all been recorded in varying numbers, together with Bewick's swans, wigeons, gadwalls, teal, pintails, garganeys, shovelers, scaups, long-tailed ducks, goldeneyes and smews.

To round off the picture, Rye Harbour is particularly rich in invertebrate life, being one of the most important sites in Sussex, and the species list includes some national rarities. Among the mammals, bats are numerous, while stoats, weasels, minks, hares, rabbits, and a collection of mice, shrews and voles may all be seen on land, while off shore porpoises and seals are occasionally sighted. Although the common frog itself has not been recorded, the marsh frog is a resident, and there are a few common toads.

Fore Wood RSPB Reserve

Managing body   RSPB.
Access   TQ 7613. Near Crowhurst. Road to Crowhurst off A2100 Battle –
Hastings road. Parking at village hall by church 400 yards downhill from
reserve entrance.
Other information   Access at all times. Leaflet.

The RSPB's 135 acre Fore Wood Reserve near Crowhurst in East
Sussex is not one of the most spectacular in terms of bird-life, but it
does give birdwatchers the opportunity of seeing most of the
species one would expect to find in a southern deciduous
woodland. Moreover, it has plenty to attract the discerning
ornithologist who is interested not just in seeing the birds, but in
seeing and understanding how a woodland of this type is managed
to provide the best possible conditions for birds and for other
wildlife.

A nature trail guide is available from a dispenser on the reserve;
this gives a description of the mile and a half walk, together with its
eighteen points of interest. A short-cut is also shown, which
roughly halves the route.

Fore Wood was bought by the RSPB in 1976. It was then a
neglected coppice that had not been managed for 30 years. It
consisted of some dense stands of oakwood, with smaller groups
and single oaks scattered throughout and the bulk of the area
divided, in more or less equal proportions, between hornbeam
and sweet chestnut. The former grew on the heavier clay soil of the
higher ground, while the slopes of the undulating land with their
more sandy soils were dominated by the latter. The extremely
steep-sided valleys or 'ghylls' with streams running along their
bottoms provide a favourable habitat for alders.

Because the wood had been neglected, it was neither one thing
nor the other – neither coppice nor mature woodland – and had
become very heavily shaded, lacking in ground cover and relatively
poor in bird-life; there were a number of species such as the tits
and tree-creepers, but hardly any warblers or wrens. Management
has, therefore, been directed towards providing habitats to attract a
greater diversity, not just of birds, but of wildlife generally. This is
being done, as explained in the nature trail guide, by opening up
the woodland, creating glades and rides, making a pond and
beginning once more to manage the coppiced areas in the
traditional ways.

The first point we came to on the trail was a ghyll – a surprisingly
steep-sided ravine in the soft sandstone – with a waterfall running

over a lip of harder sandstone and dropping down into the stream below. This dark, damp area is full of mosses, ferns, lichens and liverworts, including some rare species, and has been scheduled as an SSSI. A pair of grey wagtails nested below the waterfall in 1981.

The guide next drew our attention to the contrasting types of woodland on either side of the path. On the left, the neglected coppice consists mostly of rather poor specimens of hornbeam, with little in the way of understorey to offer cover for birds. On the right, vigorous thinning has taken place, with eighty per cent of the spindly trees being removed in 1978. The resulting light and space has allowed the remainder to develop into bigger and better specimens; fresh growth has arisen from the cut stumps, and bramble, quite dense in places, provides nesting sites and food for wrens, dunnocks and blackcaps. The seeds of the hornbeam are much favoured by hawfinches, several pairs of which breed in the reserve each year.

A little further along the path is the site of one of the many nest boxes which have been distributed throughout the wood. The smaller ones are used extensively by great and blue tits, to a lesser extent by coal and marsh tits and nuthatches, while the larger ones are occupied by starlings, great spotted woodpeckers and tawny owls. According to the guide, some are also used as winter roosts by tits and woodmice.

The guide also points out the necessity of leaving both fallen and standing dead trees, offering habitats for insects, which in turn provide food for birds such as woodpeckers. Fungi also grow on rotten wood, and, most importantly, eventual decomposition of the wood returns nutrients to the soil.

The trail at this stage was taking us along one of the many rides in the reserve – narrow path-like clearings which have the dual purpose of allowing access by tractors and of providing the woodland-edge habitat beloved of willow and garden warblers, wrens, blackcaps and cuckoos. The success of the introduction of the rides may be judged from the fact that the number of nesting warblers has risen from four pairs in 1979 to thirty-five in 1981. These smaller birds do, however, need to keep on constant alert along the rides, as a pair of sparrow-hawks nest in the wood and fly along these pathways in search of prey.

At this point the short-cut route went off to the left, but we followed the longer route, coming in due course to an ivy-covered oak tree. The guide discussed briefly the disadvantages of the ivy possibly damaging the tree's growth against the undoubted advantage of its providing food for birds in winter when other sources are scarce. It also noted that in the spring it provides nesting sites for wrens, tawny owls, goldcrests and squirrels.

On the left were nine acres of woodland now being managed as coppice. Each year an acre or so is cut, and will, over about ten years, grow up through the bushy stage – at which time it is especially attractive to warblers who feed on it – to the less useful 'pole stage', when it will be cut again, and the cycle re-starts. The newly coppiced areas allow the growth of wild flowers, while the willow and garden warblers move in about two years after the initial cutting.

As we continued on the trail, the soil changed quite suddenly from the heavy clay of the hornbeam coppice to sandier soil on which sweet chestnut was growing. The latter was introduced widely in both Sussex and Kent for use as hop poles and fencing, but it is of little use to birds as it does not support many insects. The management scheme is, therefore, to clear the sweet chestnut and re-plant with native trees such as oak, hornbeam and birch.

A little further on, the trail passes along an old sunken roadway between high banks on which were growing ferns, mosses, some heather and also holly – another source of winter food and shelter. Shortly after, we came to a small pond with a couple of moorhens and mallard, which is visited in the summer and autumn by kingfishers, green sandpipers and grey wagtails. Later still, small

The management of Fore Wood, including the reintroduction of coppicing, helps provide food and nesting sites for small birds such as wrens.

flocks of wintering teal and mallard arrive. In addition to the birds, the pond supports a wide range of wildlife including breeding frogs and palmate newts, diving beetles and water boatmen, while dragon- and damselflies abound in summer.

From the pond, a short climb up the hill brought us to the end of the trail, and an interesting and very informative excursion it was, with plenty of sightings of woodland birds, and a real opportunity to see and understand how the reserve is being managed.

Pagham Harbour
Local Nature Reserve

Managing body   West Sussex County Council.
Access   SZ 8696. From A27 Chichester by-pass take B2145 towards Selsey. Reserve car-park and information centre on left, approximately 5 miles from A27, shortly after village of Sidlesham.
Other information   Information centre open Saturday and Sunday (summer), Sunday only (winter).

Pagham Harbour Local Nature Reserve in Sussex is another which is a pleasure to the ornithologist throughout the year, and also has much to offer the botanist and entomologist at the appropriate seasons. It is managed by the West Sussex County Council, who have provided a good car-park, a nature trail and a really interesting information centre with displays telling much about the reserve, and from which may be bought two excellent booklets, The Natural History of Pagham Harbour, Parts One and Two. Part One deals with birds and mammals, and Part Two with plants and the remaining animals; both are published by the Bognor Regis Natural Science Society.

The reserve consists of a total of 1,100 acres with a wide range of habitats – tidal mud-flats (the major one), shingle beach, the harbour banks and sea-walls, reed-bed and reed pools, farmland and a small amount of woodland. Some 270 species of birds have been recorded, with the spring and autumn migrations bringing their fair share of unusual and interesting specimens.

Most visitors will probably follow the Sidlesham Ferry Nature Trail from the information centre – a mile and a half walk with numbered posts corresponding with descriptive paragraphs in the available leaflet.

The first stop of importance is the hide looking across the Chichester/Selsey road to the Ferry Pool, a small expanse of water which attracts a remarkable number of birds throughout the year.

The Ferry Pool at Pagham Harbour is noted for the less common waders such as curlew sandpipers.

Forty different waders have been recorded there, with something of interest at almost any time, although spring and autumn are probably the best. It is noted for the less common waders such as curlew sandpipers, little stints and wood sandpipers. We saw common sandpipers, ruffs, ringed plovers, redshanks, dunlins and a lone avocet – a rare delight – although a few of these lovely birds have taken to wintering at Pagham in recent years. Ducks are also common, with small numbers of teal, shovelers, tufteds and pochards wintering, and when we visited in early summer, a stray brent goose (which must have missed the general migration back to Arctic Siberia) was there.

From the hide, the trail leads around the edge of the harbour, giving excellent views of the extensive mud-flats (almost 800 acres) which are bisected at intervals by deep channels. The salt marsh vegetation consists, as usual, of such plants as sea purslane, seablite and glasswort – some of whose seeds provide finches with food. There is also extensive growth of spartina grass. The mud itself offers shelter to the many invertebrates on which a variety of waders feed – oystercatchers, redshanks and curlews in particular being relatively common at Pagham. When we were there the two former were much in evidence.

There were also appreciable numbers of shelducks on the mud-flats, feeding on the marine molluscs, searching for them with the typical side to side sweeping of their bills. These handsome birds nest in fields on or adjacent to the reserve, usually in rabbit burrows or some other well-concealed site. The female,

Fieldfares are among the winter visitors which roost in the wetter areas of fields near Siddlesham Ferry.

exceptionally among ducks, has the same conspicuous plumage as the male and would quickly fall victim to predators if the nest were not well hidden. She alone incubates the large clutch of up to sixteen cream-coloured eggs for a month. Then, soon after hatching, she and (usually) the male lead their brood down to the nearest water – a really enchanting sight for those lucky enough to see it.

British shelducks engage in a very interesting 'moult migration' in July, when birds from all over Europe congregate in the Heligoland Bight off the German coast for their annual moult – although some (possibly from Ireland) collect in Bridgwater Bay. As this migration frequently occurs before the young are fully fledged, these youngsters band together in 'creches' and are looked after by just a few remaining adults.

During the winter the harbour plays host to many brent geese which feed principally on the alga *Enteromorpha* which grows on the mud-flats. It is noteworthy that over the last few years the numbers of grey geese, once seen in the area in appreciable numbers, have dropped into the 'rare' category. This is said to be due to the development of caravan sites, drainage and building on land they formerly grazed. The brents, however, which feed on the alga have increased in numbers considerably.

The nature trail reaches its furthest point at the Mill Pond adjacent to Sidlesham Quay. The pond, with its surrounding reed and sedge marsh, provides nesting sites for moorhens, mallard, coots, and reed and sedge warblers. From here the trail returns along a footpath flanking farm fields which are used as a high tide roost for waders from the harbour. Our visit was in early summer so there were relatively few of those about, but in winter up to 3,000 dunlins, 5,000 golden plovers, 800 lapwings and 200 curlews may be there; fieldfares, redwings, snipe, godwits and teal may also be seen – the latter in the wetter areas. The hedgerows bordering the fields are used by nesting passerines, such as the various finches.

The trail ends back at the information centre, but that is by no means all there is to be seen at Pagham. A walk in the opposite direction around the sea-wall took us down along the western side of the harbour towards its narrow mouth. This side, where a moderate amount of cover is afforded by gorse and hawthorn, is a good place during migration periods, but when we were there most interest was centred around the shingle spit at the harbour mouth. It was closed at the time because it is an important breeding site for little terns (which often feed at high tide in the channels through the mud-flats nearer the information centre), and for ringed plovers and oystercatchers. The spit and the beach area are also good vantage points at migration times. Just behind the spit at low tide, we saw a number of black-tailed godwits, dunlins, common and little terns and, to our great pleasure, a female hen harrier – a splendid climax to an absorbing day.

Pagham Harbour is also of great interest to botanists as its varied habitats are the home of a number of uncommon plants as well as a wealth of better-known ones. Of the more unusual ones mouse-tail, Danish scurvy grass, sea milkwort and subterranean trefoil are to be found. There is an impressive variety of seaweeds in the lagoons, ditches, salt marshes and other habitats; lichens, too, are well-represented, as are fungi.

Ebernoe Common

Managing body   Sussex Trust for Nature Conservation.
Access   SU 9827. Approach along minor road, 3½ miles north of Petworth, running east from A283. Car-park at church.

Ebernoe Common (Sussex Trust for Nature Conservation) is a magnificent example of ancient woodland – said to be the finest in the western Weald – and gives an excellent idea of what the original

One of the two large ponds at Ebernoe Common. It is quite easy to miss them among the dense woodland.

must have looked like. It is a woodland with majestic trees. Some areas are dominated by beech, with a very thick understorey of yew and holly; while in other areas, oak is dominant, with maple and ash.

There are two large ponds (although it is quite easy to miss them among the dense forest), some open pasture and an area of scrub. There is considerable variation of soil, ranging from sandstone to clay and limestone, and this results in a variety of plants. The reserve is very rich in butterflies, including purple emperors, silver-washed fritillaries and white admirals, as well as other insects.

As might be expected, there is a wealth of woodland birds, including nightingales. Our visit was probably too early in the year to hear or see this increasingly uncommon bird or any of the various warblers that have been recorded there, but we did see many others. A woodcock got up from under our feet as we were walking through some dense undergrowth, and we saw both great and lesser spotted woodpeckers. The large pond yielded a couple of herons and a lone Canada goose. There was the usual assortment of tits, robins, wrens and tree-creepers.

It was a sheer joy to walk through this reserve – along the many rides which criss-cross it – and to see so many really magnificent trees. It was lovely when we were there in early spring; it must be quite spectacular in autumn.

Dungeness RSPB Reserve

Managing body RSPB.
Access TR 0620. Signposted off Lydd – Dungeness road.
Other information Open all year, certain days only. Information centre. Leaflet.

The Dungeness RSPB Reserve, about twenty miles along the coast east of Rye Harbour, has much in common with its neighbour, yet is totally different in character. Dungeness, like Rye, features acres of shingle and open water, but it is on a much larger scale, with some huge banks of shingle near the visitor centre, looking as if they had been piled up by some gigantic bulldozer rather than by the forces of nature. The whole area is dominated by an indisputably man-made structure, the vast Dungeness Nuclear Power-station, a menacing pile of concrete festooned with cables connecting it with the giant pylons that stalk across the wind-swept landscape.

Dungeness is a fascinating place for birdwatchers, botanists and entomologists. Protruding out into the English Channel, this huge shingle promontory (the largest of its kind in Europe and probably in the world) acts as a landfall for migrant birds and insects. The natural and man-made lagoons and pits (fresh and salt water), the dense fringes of reeds, brambles, sallow and rushes surrounding them, and an area of scrubland with gorse, blackthorn, elder and bramble – all offer habitats for an exciting variety of birds. Surprisingly, in the bleak surroundings, there are also a number of interesting plants.

After inspecting the informative visitor centre, we made our way to the hides overlooking the Burrowes Pit – an expanse of seventy-nine acres of water which was excavated from the gravel in the 1930s and named in memory of Robert Burrowes, who gave the area to the RSPB in 1930. It was, in fact, the Society's first reserve.

As we opened the flaps in the first hide we were immediately confronted with a sky full of gulls and terns which had taken to the air from the surface of the water and from the small islands dotted throughout the pit. Most of the gulls were black-headed, but there were some herrings and, to our delight, at least one common gull – the reserve being well known as the only regular breeding station for the latter, with a regular population of about twelve pairs.

Mediterranean gulls can also be seen and two pairs bred in 1981.

We saw three species of terns – Arctic, common and Sandwich – the latter have bred at Dungeness for many years. We could not spot any of the little terns that gave us such pleasure at Rye Harbour, although they do breed in small numbers in the Dungeness area.

Moving on to the next hide, we had a better view of the terns, which had by now subsided, and an excellent close-up of several turnstones, foraging around the water's edge, as well as a lone common sandpiper that popped in and out of the vegetation. A few dunlins were pecking away on one of the islands, and of the wildfowl (not the right time of the year for any great numbers) we saw some pochards, tufted ducks and mallard.

The third hide provided us with great interest, excitement and amusement. As we peered out, we saw a pair of Canada geese emerge from behind a shingle bank and make their way across the open area of pebbles, followed by one quite sizeable gosling, then two, three, four, five, six ... smaller youngsters. We thought that was it – but no! After a short pause, more emerged, and still more, until finally we counted fourteen – all marching purposefully across the shingle, their huge feet giving them the appearance of wearing over-large 'wellies'. It was a priceless sight. The larger gosling clearly belonged to someone else and was probably being fostered, but the remainder were, apparently, all one brood. We returned to the same hide later on, and saw the large family had settled down on the grassy verge of the pit, so we had a closer look at them.

It was from this last hide that we had perhaps our best 'sighting' of the day. When we arrived, other birdwatchers were talking about a black-necked grebe they had seen earlier in the day. Naturally, we were keen to see it, but a careful scanning of the area revealed nothing even remotely like it. It was not until we returned later that we glimpsed what might have been the grebe. Right over on the far side of the pit, nearer to the power-station, was an island – quite long and covered with scrub. Between the bushes, we thought we could see the elusive bird swimming quietly backwards and forwards. But would it come out into the open so we could be sure? Of course not! However patience must be part of a birdwatcher's make-up and finally ours was rewarded. The shy bird swam into view and we had a clear, if distant, view.

We could see quite plainly the lovely little bird's fan-shaped golden crest, the black neck and upper back plumage and a glimpse of the chestnut sides. We could also distinguish the slight up-turning of the bill – a point that helps separate it from the Slavonian grebe. The two breeds are much more difficult to separate in winter plumage, when, in addition to the curved bill,

A pair of Canada geese with fourteen goslings, marching purposefully across the shingle, is our abiding memory of Dungeness.

the black-necked has a higher forehead than the Slavonian, more white on the wing when in flight and more white on the nape of the neck – very small, exceedingly difficult points to determine, especially when, as invariably happens, the two species cannot be directly compared.

In winter, the water and its surroundings attract large numbers of wildfowl, including wigeons, gadwalls, shovelers, goldeneyes, goosanders and smews, in addition to red-necked, black-necked and Slavonian grebes. The water's edge attracts passage waders such as green and wood sandpipers, while grey plovers, dunlins and oystercatchers roost.

In addition to the Burrowes Pit, there are also the Fossil Pits, which include two stretches of water believed to be the only areas in the world of natural fresh water in shingle. Much of the surrounding area is heavily overgrown with sallow, and several unusual plants can be found – marsh fern, the hop and saw sedges and the intriguing jointed rush, the internal horizontal joints of which can be felt by running the finger down the stem.

It is this area which gives Dungeness such a reputation for migrant birds. On a good day, it is said to be truly 'alive' with birds – willow warblers, spotted flycatchers and chiffchaffs occur in quite extraordinary numbers, while sightings of less common birds such as wrynecks, bluethroats and black terns occur almost every year. Nesting species around the Fossil Pits include the reed bunting, sedge and reed warblers, little grebe, shelduck, water rail and shoveler.

From the hides, we followed the marked trail around the reserve along wide shingle pathways guarded on both sides by high shingle banks – a section of the reserve not noted for easy walking conditions, particularly on a hot day! Scattered round were clumps of the prostrate form of broom that has developed at Dungeness – the bright yellow flowers making really brilliant splashes of colour against the shingle. Soon the shingle merged into stony grassland with gorse bushes, bramble and blackthorn scrub. Nesting species in this area include the yellowhammer, whitethroat, linnet and partridge. On our visit, reed buntings were there in profusion.

Dungeness is also home to newts and toads, and, interestingly, marsh frogs have eliminated the common frog. Just eight of these amphibians were imported from south-east Europe in 1935 and released onto Romney Marsh. They quickly spread, bred and reached the reserve, where they have been extremely successful – their loud voices giving away their presence in summer.

The reserve is also of importance for both breeding and migrant insects, with a remarkable number of hawk moths being recorded – privet, pole, elephant and small elephant all being listed as breeding, while visiting species include the hummingbird and the convolvulus. Migrant butterflies include the red admiral, peacock, clouded yellow and, very occasionally, the rare pale clouded yellow.

Hothfield Common

Managing body   Kent Trust for Nature Conservation/Ashford Borough Council.
Access   TQ 9746. Turn off A20 on minor road to Hothfield village. Car-park near reserve entrance about 300 yards along, on right.
Other information   Leaflet available from Trust: phone Medway 362561.

This is a very attractive area of woodland, heathland and bog – not primarily a bird reserve, but with over sixty species recorded and thirty-five breeding. The heathland and bog are unusual in Kent so the reserve is being managed to safeguard them for the future. There is a nature trail covering a comprehensive area of the reserve, and a number of other paths through the common for the more energetic.

The nature trail at Hothfield Common led up to mature woodland at Foxenhill, with beech, oak, and pine.

A leaflet obtainable from the Kent Trust for Nature Conservation explains how the rather unusual formation of the reserve has occurred. The common is on a plateau in the Folkestone Sands: water drained from it penetrates the Sands, but, when it reaches the underlying impenetrable Sandgate Beds, it emerges as acid springs. In the course of time, peat has accumulated in some of the shallow valleys, and the four peat mires all drain into a stream which empties into the Great Stour river.

At one time, heathers grew on the drier, raised ground between the valleys, and trees were found on the knolls – but this pattern was upset in 1949 when a huge fire burned for several days, igniting some of the peat in the valley bogs or mires. The area of ash which remained after the fire acted as a seedbed and soon small trees such as birch and willow invaded, and with no grazing by commoners' animals or by rabbits (the latter due to myxomatosis), bracken also spread.

Today, the management of the reserve is devoted to maintaining and reclaiming the heathland and the mires, with bracken and birch being systematically removed. At the edges of the common, the woodland, which is quite extensive and very beautiful, is being allowed to develop naturally, particularly as it provides nesting and feeding sites for birds and other animals.

The nature trail led us initially through mixed woodland of birch, small oaks and sycamore, where a good variety of woodland birds may be seen. We saw blackcaps and chiffchaffs, nuthatches and tree-creepers. This type of wood soon gave way to more mature woodland, as we went up the incline to Foxenhill, where there was beech, oak and pine, with some sweet chestnut. Birds included green woodpeckers, tree-creepers and some spotted flycatchers. On the warm, summer's day it was really lovely, with the coolness of the woodland depths and the brightness of the sun shining on the trees at the wood's edge.

From the knoll, the path took us down through some birch scrub towards the heathland and bog area. The path led via a wooden causeway, across the centre of the largest bog, and gave us a good opportunity of inspecting the bog plants – sphagnum, heath milkwort, cotton grass and the rare (in Kent) round-leaved sundew. Below the bogs are more marshy areas, with many wetland plants such as marsh bedstraw, yellow iris, water mint and devil's-bit scabious – all of which may be seen at various times. The scrubby area offers food and cover for some of the passerines, such as willow and garden warblers, while sedge warblers may be heard and seen in the thickets. We saw none of the adders, grass snakes or the common lizards which are found on the reserve.

The remainder of the nature trail consisted of pleasant walks through semi-mature woodland, before arriving back at the starting place by the entrance.

Stodmarsh National Nature Reserve

Managing body NCC.
Access TR 2261. Take A257 east from Canterbury towards Sandwich. After a mile turn left on unclassified road to Stodmarsh. In village, turn left into lane after Red Lion, to car-park.
Other information Open all year. Leaflets available in hut in car-park.

Stodmarsh is one of those exciting reserves where you feel you might see almost anything at any time; it is a superb place for birdwatchers. Situated on the south bank of the River Stour, it is an area of about 400 acres of alluvial marshland with huge reed-beds, partially flooded meadows and shallow lagoons, formed largely as the result of land subsidence over underground coal mines. Running through the reserve is the Lampen Wall, a flood protection barrier, and from the pathway along the top of this, there are excellent views of the various habitats. A descriptive leaflet with a map is available from the Nature Conservancy Council hut in the small car-park at the entrance to the reserve.

The rough roadway which leads to the main area of the reserve is lined by trees and scrub, with a fair selection of small birds such as tits, robins, nuthatches and wrens. At the start of the Lampen Wall, we heard and saw a number of reed buntings, clinging to the stems of the reeds which dominate the swamp and fringe the dykes running along and through the vast reed-beds. The water of the dykes contains a wide range of aquatic plants – great spearwort, greater bladder wort, great water dock, bog bean, frogbit and pond sedge.

We soon came to an area of open lagoon, and there we caught a glimpse of a male bearded tit, clinging to the stem of a reed, so we waited quietly and soon had a really good view of this elusive and handsome bird. On the water of the lagoon itself were any number of great crested grebes, mallard and tufted ducks.

Swallows and martins were quite common, but if there is one bird above all others that we shall always associate with Stodmarsh, it is the swift. There were hundreds of them, wheeling and diving in pursuit of insects, calling loudly as they did so. And what remarkable birds they are! They arrive in Britain from central and southern Africa later than most other migrants, about the end of April, and leave earlier, before the end of August. During their eight

At Stodmarsh, the waters of the dykes which run through the vast reed-beds contain a wide range of aquatic plants.

or nine months absence from Britain they are, incredibly, on the wing continuously – feeding, drinking and even sleeping in flight. This is, it seems, achieved by rising high in the sky on air currents and taking short naps before coming to again and regaining height.

Swifts are well-adapted to their aerial, insect-catching life. Their legs are tiny, with four small forward-pointing and exceedingly sharp claws which help them cling on to vertical surfaces such as house walls. By this means they can clamber into their nests which are often under eaves. Nesting material – grass, straw and feathers – is picked up in flight and cemented into a small cup with saliva; mating either takes place there or on the wing. Only two or three elongated eggs are laid, and are incubated for about eighteen days. The eggs are unusually resistent to chilling, as in bad weather they are left for appreciable periods while the parents scavenge far and wide for food. The young spend up to eight weeks in the nest and may be left for several days, their night temperature falling from 101 degrees to the low 70s without ill-effect. The parents collect insect food on the wing – making full use of their large gape – glueing the insects together into a ball with sticky saliva and storing it in their throat pouch.

A few small hawthorn bushes were dotted along the wall at intervals, in some of which were small flocks of goldfinches, an occasional greenfinch and a few little bands of long-tailed tits. A little further along on the left, an even larger expanse of open water came into view, on which we counted another seven or eight great crested grebes and a number of coots and tufted ducks, with some moorhens skulking about on the lagoon edges. Garganeys, shelducks and shovelers all breed on the reserve. For some time we watched a lone common tern wheeling low over the water and perching on a post some way out from the shore.

On the other side of the wall, among the reeds, a brief flash of a chestnut-coloured bird, accompanied by a startlingly loud song told us that yet another rarity, the Cetti's warbler, was present. Later on we had a better view of one, which was a treat, as they have only recently colonised the reserve. We also heard a Savi's warbler and a grasshopper warbler – it really is a marvellous place for these little birds. We did not, however, see any of those other inhabitants of the reed-bed – the bitterns.

One of the delights of Stodmarsh is that each bend in the path reveals a different piece of scenery: a small alder and willow fringed pool with mallard on it, a dense patch of greater reed mace, and, further on, a glimpse through the thick scrub of the River Stour. Further on still, the river runs alongside the path.

At the far end of the reserve is a large expanse of wet meadowland, where we saw and heard drumming snipe and lapwings, and where ruff and black-tailed godwits are sometimes seen. In winter, the reserve is a haven for a variety of wildfowl, with geese and swans not uncommon, together with hen harriers, marsh harriers, and even the occasional osprey.

It is not just for the birdwatcher that Stodmarsh is such a rewarding place. As might be expected, the reserve has an enormous range of water plants. In addition to those already mentioned, mare's-tail and sea-club rush may be found in the meadows, and in one of the drier areas, according to the reserve leaflet, the very local species, dittander, is found. It is a member of the Cruciferae family, and is also, I believe, known as broad-leaved pepperwort.

The reserve leaflet also gives an interesting outline of how the reserve is managed. The maintenance of the marshland requires careful control of the water-levels, which is carried out with the co-operation of the Southern Water Authority. The quality of the reed-beds is maintained by cutting a selected area each year, to improve its growth and to prevent an accumulation of leaf litter. The cut reed is used for thatching. The meadows are grazed by cattle, so the natural succession to scrubland that would otherwise take place is controlled.

We found this reserve absolutely packed with interest and a delightful place to visit. Walking is easy, although the track is probably not suitable for wheelchairs.

Farlington Marshes

Managing body   Hampshire and Isle of Wight Naturalists' Trust.
Access   SU 6804. Along gravel track off south-east quadrant (main sign to Southsea) of A27/A2030 roundabout, under M27 flyover. Parking space limited.
Other information   Booklet available: 8 Market Place, Romsey, Hampshire.

Farlington Marshes reserve on Langstone Harbour near Portsmouth is one of the most exciting places for birdwatchers along the south coast, especially in winter. The reserve consists of 300 acres of wetland in the north-west corner of Langstone Harbour. It is a Local Nature Reserve of great ornithological and botanical interest, leased to the Hampshire and Isle of Wight Naturalists' Trust by Portsmouth City Council, and designated an SSSI. It is a roughly triangular peninsula bordered on two sides by a sea-wall, from which excellent views of much of Langstone Harbour can be obtained, and on the third side by the M27 motorway. Most of the remainder of the harbour is an important RSPB reserve.

Much of what is now Farlington Marshes reserve was reclaimed during the eighteenth century from salt marsh islands and mud-flats, although there is evidence of earlier reclamation. A large proportion of the reclaimed land has been used continuously up to and including the present day for grazing, and this, as the informative booklet available from the reserve warden remarks,

Many typical birds, such as greenfinches, are found in the areas of dense scrub at Farlington.

'has resulted in the survival of a type of scenery which was once typical of the land bordering the shores of Langstone Harbour; that is, rough pasture intersected by drainage ditches and scattered ponds and wet areas sometimes liable to flooding by winter rain and occasionally by exceptionally high tides'.

As we arrived at the reserve entrance, we were greeted with the incredible sight of a great cloud of birds in the air over the central marshes – a cloud that wheeled and shimmered in the sunlight before sinking out of sight behind the big banks. It was made up of thousands of waders who use the marsh as a roost while waiting for the tide to recede and expose the mud-flats of the harbour where they feed.

From the entrance, in the north-west corner, we made our way to the first of the three principal habitats into which the reserve can be roughly divided. This is an area of rough grassland covered with many clumps of dense scrub, consisting of gorse, bramble, hawthorn and blackthorn interspersed with ponds and some bomb craters. A number of birds typical of hedges and scrub are present, including resident greenfinches, dunnocks and wrens – all of which we saw. Summer nesting visitors include whitethroats, lesser whitethroats, blackcaps and willow warblers – but, as we were there in winter, we did not see them. We did, however, see some of the redwings, which together with fieldfares feed on the blackthorn berries (most of these two species of birds are from Scandinavia).

The area is particularly interesting in spring and autumn, containing an unusually high number of grasses (approximately one third of all the British species) as well as a good selection of other scarce plants including the hairy buttercup. There are a number of water plants, including the lesser reed mace, which is found in two of the three ponds. The distribution of these water plants depends largely on the salinity of the water, as does that of water animals. This is illustrated in the three bomb craters; in the two with fresh water, toads and newts are found, while in the more brackish one there are decapod shrimps. Frogs are quite common on the reserve as a whole and steps are being taken to protect them.

The rough pasture and scrub give way, behind the high banks, to the second of the habitats, which is certainly one of the most interesting. It consists of a freshwater stream flowing along the line of an earlier saltwater creek and leading into a large lagoon. Around these two stretches are a number of salt-tolerant plants – the salt is retained in the soil from the former creek. Mud rush, glasswort and salt marsh grass may be seen in addition to reeds, glaucous bulrush, sea-club rush and sea asters, all of which can survive the water-logged conditions and frequent flooding. In 1963, the Naturalists' Trust erected a mile-long fence along the stream and one side of the lagoon to protect it from the grazing cattle which are turned out on the rest of the reserve. This is to protect the reed-beds and allow them to extend.

The lagoon is a haven for significant numbers of wildfowl and other birds. We saw plenty of teal, wigeon, shovelers and shelducks, and little grebes, moorhens and coots are breeding. In the reed-beds, sedge and reed warblers nest, and when we were there we caught brief glimpses of a water rail along the edge of the reeds. We saw a number of snipe, but not the rarer Jack snipe of which there are small numbers on the reserve.

One of the most encouraging developments over the last twenty years has been the visits, now regular, of bearded tits, which winter among the reed-beds; we saw some of these. Ringing has shown that they come from the RSPB reserves at Minsmere and Walberswick; Farlington obviously provides these birds, which are very vulnerable to severe weather, with a welcome refuge from the rigours of the East Anglian coast.

The remainder of the reserve is taken up with the third habitat, open marshland, which provides rough pasture for the cattle. In

We caught some brief glimpses of a water rail along the edge of the
reeds in the lagoon at Farlington.

this area are the remains of some of the creeks that formerly wound
round the salt marsh islands; one of these old creeks has been
flooded to provide a large area of fresh water attractive to ducks
and to some of the rare waders such as ruffs, greenshanks and
stints. Much of the marsh is the roost for the thousands of waders
and wildfowl that make Langstone Harbour one of the most
important wintering sites in the south.

At high tides, when the mud-flats are flooded, the central area is a
marvellous sight – with thousands of dunlins, large numbers of
oystercatchers, curlews, redshanks, bar-tailed godwits and grey
plovers. It is not possible to see many of them at very close quarters
as they wisely keep to the centre of the marsh from which the
public are excluded – but with good binoculars or a telescope most
of them can be picked out. Of special interest are the numbers of
black-tailed godwits – with between ten and fifteen per cent of the
British wintering population coming to Langstone.

Ringing at Farlington has shown that the wintering dunlins breed in Siberia, then follow a migration route through the Baltic and down the coast to the Low Countries. They may moult in Holland, or cross to the Wash, dispersing from there to other parts of Britain.

Predators at Farlington include the carrion crow and kestrel – both of which we saw. We were also exceptionally lucky to see a pair of short-eared owls which got up quite close to us over the marsh as we were walking along the sea-wall. They feed chiefly on long-tailed voles.

One of the great features of Farlington – and indeed of Langstone Harbour as a whole – are the huge numbers of dark-bellied brent geese that winter there. Arriving from their Arctic Siberian breeding grounds around October, the total numbers of these handsome birds in the harbour may exceed 60,000 – a far cry from the early 1950s when there were less than 100 and the breed was in real danger of extinction. During the winter the geese may be seen almost anywhere around the harbour, and they graze in small parties all over the marshes at high tide before returning to the sea to feed on the green alga, Enteromorpha.

There were hundreds of them there during our visit, with skeins of them strung out across the sky as they moved from place to place. As the tide receded the evocative sound of their continuous honking grew fainter as they moved further away from the sea-wall in search of food. They leave for the return flight to their breeding grounds in March – much to the relief of farmers from Farlington to Chichester, on whose grass and winter crops the birds also feed, and to whom, indeed, they are becoming quite a serious pest.

The sea-wall, which encircles much of the reserve, is a fine vantage point from which to see the birds of the harbour itself. In addition to the waders and the geese, black-necked grebes, red-breasted mergansers and large numbers of goldeneyes may be seen off shore. The wall itself provides a habitat for a number of interesting plants. On sections of the seaward-facing surface where there are remains of the original construction of flint and chalk held together by timber, salt marsh plants such as sea wormwood and sea purslane, golden samphire and sea beet find a foothold. On the inward-facing surfaces, slender haresear and grass vetchling may be found.

Altogether, Farlington Marshes provides a wealth of interesting species for ornithologist and botanist alike and – most important of all – it provides a refuge for vast numbers of waders and wildfowl, all of which can be seen just a very short distance from where heavy traffic hurtles noisily along the motorway.

South-west England

Brownsea Island

Managing body   Dorset Naturalists' Trust.
Access   SZ 0388. By boat only from Sandbanks or Poole Quay.
Other information   Daily guided tours. Open April – September only.

Brownsea Island, lying at the entrance to Poole Harbour in Dorset, has two claims to fame. Firstly, it is known world-wide as the site of Sir Robert Baden-Powell's first camp for boys, which led to the founding of the Boy Scout movement. Secondly, it is known for its wildlife, particularly for the nature reserve at the eastern end of the island, which is managed by the Dorset Naturalists' Trust.

It is reached by boat from either of two boarding points on Poole harbour, and the trip across, especially the one from Poole Quay, may give the visitor an early sight of some of the bird-life that abounds in the harbour itself. We have visited it a number of times, both in summer and winter – but winter visits are restricted to members of the Dorset Naturalists' Trust. Brownsea Island, owned by the National Trust, is open to the public from April until September, and there are regular guided tours of the nature reserve.

The recent history of the island is interesting and has a considerable bearing on the wildlife to be seen. It is a mile and a half long and half a mile wide, and was managed for many years as a country estate, with arable, woodlands and a spread of daffodil fields. In 1927 it was acquired by Mrs Bonham-Christie, who, with the best of intentions as far as the wildlife was concerned, 'returned it to nature'. The result of this was that it very soon became a real wilderness of impenetrable rhododendron, gorse, bramble, birch and pine. The sea-birds enjoyed it, as an extensive seawater lagoon formed when the sea-wall was breached and the water meadows were flooded. After Mrs Bonham-Christie's death, the island became the property of the National Trust and some time later, 240 acres of its total of about 500 was leased to the Dorset Naturalists' Trust, who are doing a magnificent job of managing the reserve so formed.

On our most recent visit, during the winter, we were lucky in seeing a number of birds before we actually landed – including mergansers, goldeneyes, great crested grebes, brent geese, wigeons and teal, in addition to some of the many cormorants which are features not just of the island but of Poole Harbour. A solitary guillimot did not look particularly well and was possibly an oiled bird.

We landed at the Quay, and walked along the road past the public hide, which is open throughout the summer and gives good views over the lagoon, normally full of sea-birds and waders. Along the edge of the road are a number of trees – beech, Monterey pine, alder willow and sycamore – and it was only a matter of a very few minutes before we heard the extraordinary call of the peacocks which are such a feature of the island. They parade around in large numbers on the grassy area in front of the church, and also range widely over the non-reserve part of the island, nesting and raising their rather ungainly young. The sight of the male bird displaying is almost worth a visit to Brownsea on its own! The grassy area has in and around it a very interesting collection of trees – scarlet oak, deodar, cedar and a mulberry that was planted near the church by Lady Baden-Powell in 1963.

In this account, I am going to depart slightly from the usual plan of describing the reserve itself, and describe what we saw throughout our tour of the island, because anyone who visits Brownsea and only sees the reserve is likely to miss much of interest.

On this visit, as on most, we did not go immediately to the reserve, but set off up the hill towards the south cliff by way of fields which, in the spring, are a mass of daffodils, and then through some pine-dotted heathland to a point overlooking the harbour. On the way we saw some ivy that had been browsed by some of the small herd of Sika deer that, within the last few years, have swum over from the mainland and settled on the island.

On the cliff, we looked out across the harbour – a fine view – and careful searching revealed a number of sea-birds, including a pair of eiders, more of the goldeneyes that regularly winter around the harbour, more mergansers (they too winter in the harbour in significant numbers) and a red-necked grebe. Oystercatchers were busy on the shore below and, just as we were about to leave, a flock of grey plovers flew over, followed by a wheeling, turning mass of dunlins – probably going out to the feeding grounds on the falling tide.

We could have continued our walk further round the coast accompanied by the ubiquitous peacocks, but instead we circled back to the reserve. Just near it, we were lucky to have a good look

Wall charts in the villa on Brownsea Island show that knots seen on the island have been recovered in Germany.

at one of the island's famous breeding population of about sixty red squirrels. This was an adult – it was the wrong time to see the young, of which there are two broods annually, most commonly seen in May and September. The population is being watched carefully and with some concern, as the numbers now have not increased for ten years, and it is felt that their survival as a breeding colony may be in doubt if they decrease below the present numbers. Food is not a problem for them on Brownsea, as they have both Scots and Maritime pine (the latter in its only British station), so that if one fails, the other is on hand.

On the left as we entered the reserve was quite an extensive area of reed-bed, and somewhere in the distance we heard the harsh call of a water rail – a number are winter visitors and one or two pairs may breed. On our right, a thick bank of scrub lay between us and the lagoon, but we headed straight for the warden's villa to eat our packed lunch and to look around the museum which gives a very good idea of what may be seen on the island. Of special interest are the wall charts that show the origin and destinations of the migratory birds seen on the island. For instance, knots from Brownsea have been recovered in Germany, while the black-tailed godwits come from Iceland and the curlews 'commute' between the island and France, also travelling from Finland and Sweden.

From the villa we went along the walk to the far eastern end of the island which houses the second largest heronry in Britain, with nearly 100 nests at present. On our way we passed one of the two freshwater lakes, which is biologically 'dead' because of its extreme acidity, but which the Trust is trying to improve, at least around the margins, by encouraging molinia and heather to grow.

The heronry is an impressive sight, and we were able to have a good look at it in the absence of the birds; it is out of bounds during the breeding season. There are dozens of nests perched high in the pine trees, and all are carefully monitored during the season. The numbers of nesting attempts and the numbers of chicks reared are recorded.

Throughout the reserve we were tremendously impressed with the work that is being done by volunteers in clearing the rhododendron 'jungle'. It is the most tenacious of plants, and clearing it is an enormous task.

We made our way back towards the *pièce de résistance* of the reserve – the hide overlooking the lagoon. On our way we were fortunate to see, from the path on the ridge high above the beach, a peregrine sitting quietly on a log in a grassy area. We were some distance away, but we had a wonderful view of him through binoculars; although we waited for quite some time he did not move. The lagoon hide gives splendid views of the large areas of non-tidal water which holds an exciting variety of birds at all times of the year. This time there was the unforgettable sight of about twenty-four avocets – a species that has been wintering on the reserve regularly for a few years now. About 1,200 dunlins were present, together with a few pintails, some gadwalls, a collection of oystercatchers, redshanks, teal, wigeons, cormorants and a single curlew. The small islands, which during the summer provide nesting sites for common and Sandwich terns, were almost deserted, except for the dunlins.

Brownsea has an impressive list of over 200 birds – some of them rare passage migrants – and at the appropriate times a full range of waders and wildfowl are common; while the reed-beds, woods, alder and willow carr hold reed and sedge warblers, goldcrests, wrens and blackcaps. The joy about Brownsea is that you can never be sure what you might see at any time. One visit we paid coincided with reports of a spoonbill (a number have been seen over the years) and although we spoke to several people who had seen it, it was another of those 'Oh, you've just missed it' days, and we never actually did see it!

Arne RSPB Reserve

Managing body   RSPB.
Access   SY 9888. From A351 Wareham – Swanage road turn left in Stoborough village, follow signposts to Arne.
Other information   Leaflet available from RSPB. Escorted walks April – August, certain days only. Permits from Sydale, Arne, Wareham, BH20 5BJ in advance. Access to Shipstal Point from car-park all year.

The Arne Peninsula, in the north-west of Poole Harbour, contains one of the largest areas of lowland heath in Britain, and about 1,200 acres are now owned by the RSPB. In addition to the heath there are several other important habitats, including conifer and deciduous woodland, marsh, reed swamp and salt marsh.

The reserve is important for one bird above all others – the rare Dartford warbler – which is confined to the heathlands of Dorset and Hampshire, where it is at the northern and eastern limits of its range. It is notoriously vulnerable to severe winters, and the small population was all but wiped out in the big freeze of 1962/63. Only about ten pairs were known to have survived, of which two were on Arne, but the population has increased since then.

This elusive little bird, one of the two non-migrants among British warblers, is exceptionally difficult to see, and although we have seen them at various times in the nearby New Forest, we did not see one at Arne. They can be seen most often when they perch briefly on top of a gorse bush – the male singing loudly, with its long tail flicking up and down. They quickly fly off, with bouncing flight, and disappear into the lower parts of the surrounding vegetation.

Dartford warblers are very dark in colour – the male having dark brown upper parts and slate grey head, with deep red, almost wine-coloured underparts. The head is lighter grey in summer. The female is a little more brown in colour overall. The nest, which is found in the lowest branches of the bushes, is built mostly by the female, who raises two or even three broods, sharing incubation with the male. Dartford warblers feed on beetles, flies and caterpillars and, in the autumn, blackberries.

Only part of the reserve at Arne is open to the public throughout the year. The remainder can only be viewed on escorted walks from April through until August; permits for these must be obtained in advance. The walk to Shipstal Point and to a hide overlooking the salt marshes is well worth taking, particularly in winter when a number of sea ducks can be seen off shore, and some of the resident birds may be seen *en route*.

We followed the path to the beach and enjoyed a walk along it. In the channel, we saw a number of mergansers and goldeneyes, but none of the pintails, teal, or great crested grebes that might have been expected at that time of the year. In the summer, common, little and Sandwich terns are often seen.

From the beach we re-traced our steps to a path which led to a hide overlooking part of the salt marshes. The path passed through an area of woodland – some of which was pine (Scots and one or two Maritime) and silver birch. Here we saw some of the expected woodland birds such as tits, tree-creepers and goldcrests – the latter in evidence by sound rather than by sight. During migration times, redstarts, pied and spotted flycatchers, sparrow-hawks, kestrels and buzzards may also be seen in this part of the reserve.

The extensive salt marshes and mud-flats provide food and shelter for large numbers of waders – curlews, redshanks, dunlins, oystercatchers and lapwings in winter; while at migration times, whimbrels, bar-tailed godwits, grey plovers, greenshanks and spotted redshanks appear to find the area particularly attractive, with flocks of up to 100 seen. In spring, more than 600 black-tailed godwits have been recorded.

We did not see very much from the hide, just a few redshanks, but when we walked further round to a point overlooking more of the mud-flats, there were dozens of birds, including bar-tailed

The extensive salt marshes and mud-flats at Arne provide food and shelter for large numbers of waders, including bar-tailed godwits.

godwits, curlews and dunlins.

We could not gain access to the heathland areas when we were there in late autumn, but meadow pipits, stonechats, linnets, yellowhammers, cuckoos and nightjars are regularly seen in some numbers. Hen harriers are frequent visitors in winter. The reed-beds abound with reed buntings and warblers, moorhens, mallard, teal and water rails, and bearded tits have recently begun to breed in the marshy areas.

With such a variety of habitats, it is not surprising that there is a diversity of other animals on the reserve, including roe and Sika deer, badgers, common, pygmy and water shrews, harvest mice, all six British reptiles and palmate newts. There are many species of insects, some of relatively local distribution and some interesting migrant species due to Arne's proximity to continental Europe. Local moth species include Kent black arches, several species of footmen, and the pink hawk moth. Of great interest among the grasshoppers to be found is the heath – which is confined to Purbeck – and a number of dragonflies comparatively scarce in the rest of Britain, are also here. Among the many plants typical of heath and bogland, the local Dorset heath is found.

Radipole Lake RSPB Reserve

Managing body   RSPB.
Access   SY 6880. Swannery car-park in Weymouth town centre.
Other information   Visitor centre open all week mid-June – mid-September, weekends all year. Warden: 52 Goldcroft Road, Weymouth, Dorset.

Radipole Lake is one of the most surprising of bird reserves, situated, as it is, right in the heart of the town of Weymouth in Dorset. It adjoins one of the town's principal car-parks, but remarkably, a total of over 250 species of birds have been recorded, with well over 40 breeding. Even more satisfying is the fact that in the last 20 years the huge reed-beds have attracted two important new breeding species – bearded tits in 1964 and Cetti's warblers in 1976 – both now well-established, albeit in small numbers.

The reserve is owned by the Weymouth and Portland Borough Council and is leased to the RSPB who manage it. It has been designated an SSSI. Near the entrance is a coloured map of the reserve, with a brief description telling visitors that the area was formerly the estuary of the River Wey, and that until 1924 the sea flowed up to the village of Radipole. In 1924, Westham Bridge was constructed with tide flaps and sluices, forming a lake which, since then, has gradually become fresh water.

Radipole Lake Reserve is notably well organised and easily accessible, especially for the physically and visually handicapped. Paths suitable for wheelchairs have been laid throughout, there is a tap rail for the blind, and for all visitors there are a number of listening posts with recorded commentaries on various aspects of the reserve and its birds. The visitor centre is very well laid out and informative, and offers excellent viewing over an important area of the lake.

Radipole, with its 200 acres of open water (coming from the River Wey which runs through it), reed-beds, dry grassland and bushy scrub, is another delightful reserve where there is something of interest throughout the year. In winter, several thousand wildfowl congregate – teal, shovelers, tufteds, pochards and shelducks are common, with goldeneyes, wigeons, scaups, gadwalls and pintails less frequently seen on and around the lake. The scrubby area provides food and shelter for the resident thrushes, which are joined by over-wintering redwings and fieldfares from Scandinavia, while the reeds are used as a roost for hundreds of pied wagtails.

One of the most spectacular sights at Radipole, from late summer onwards, is the thousands of starlings which assemble on the roofs of nearby houses before coming in to roost in the reeds. Such numbers naturally attract the attention of predators, particularly sparrow-hawks and kestrels. When they appear, the whole roost takes to the air, filling the sky with birds.

Although in winter the reed-beds appear uninteresting, they are none the less acting as host to the larvae of wainscot moths and crane-flies lodged within the hollow stems, which provide food for the breeding and visiting birds in the spring and summer. The same beds really come to life in spring, with hundreds of small birds – reed and sedge warblers, grasshopper warblers, reed buntings, bearded tits, chiffchaffs, willow warblers and whitethroats – nearly all of which breed in greater or lesser numbers.

Our visit to the reserve in spring was made all the more exciting by the presence of Cetti's warblers. As we strolled around the paths, we were frequently startled by the sudden, very loud and very close song of the male. Elusive though they are, we did manage to glimpse one, with its rich chestnut upper parts and its rather dirty-grey underparts, as it sped away at the conclusion of its brief song.

These birds and their interesting habits have been carefully observed at Radipole. The males are polygamous, and to accommodate the two or three females with which they mate (although four or five are not unknown), their territories may be up

The reed-beds at Radipole Lake really come to life in the spring, with hundreds of small birds, including whitethroats.

to a quarter of a mile in length. Much of the male's time is taken up patrolling this territory. After singing briefly at one end of it, he dashes at speeds of up to forty miles per hour through the bushes to a song post at the far end to sing again there. Thus, the male plays little, if any, part in the remainder of the breeding cycle. He does not help with the incubation of the strikingly red eggs, nor feed the females, although he may occasionally feed the chicks. As a result, the female has to leave the nest every quarter of an hour or so to feed herself, and, when the eggs have been hatched, she must also do most of the feeding of the youngsters. For this reason, incubation is extended to sixteen days, and there are fourteen to sixteen days from hatching to fledging, compared with eleven to twelve days for each in the case of the reed warbler. It is interesting that the song pattern of each male is as distinctive as a fingerprint in humans, and remains constant for life. Moreover, they rival nightingales as night singers, frequently performing in May, on a fixed perch, from about 1.30 a.m. until just before dawn.

We were also fortunate in having a really good view of a water rail from the reserve centre near the bridge; these secretive birds are present throughout the year in considerable numbers, and they occasionally breed at the reserve. Another delight was the presence of great crested grebes in full breeding plumage, patrolling up and down the river. This species is also present throughout the year, a small number breeding. Other grebes recorded on the reserve include the little, and the occasional visiting Slavonian and black-necked.

Studland Heath
National Nature Reserve

Managing body   NCC.
Access   SZ 0385. From ferry road (toll) north of Studland village.
Other information   Leaflets for nature trails available on site. Warden: 0929 423453.

The Studland Heath National Nature Reserve in Dorset has an enormous amount to offer – not only to the keen birdwatcher, but to anyone interested in a variety of natural history topics. Within its 1,600 acres it offers a range of habitats – a lake, bog, woodland, heathland, beach and sand-dunes – the latter of very great interest as they show clearly how the dune system has developed and changed over the last 250 years. (Strictly speaking, the beach is not within the boundaries of the reserve, but as most people go along it to reach the start of one of the two nature trails, I shall include it.)

The reserve was established in 1962 and is situated on a promontory at the entrance of Poole Harbour. It contains two nature trails – one which is open from April until September, and a sand-dune trail which is accessible throughout the year. We visited the reserve on two separate days, but it is perfectly possible to complete both nature trails within a single day. However, there is so much to see that many days could be spent there very profitably.

We decided to follow the dune trail first, and, leaving the car-park, walked towards the edge of the cliff overlooking Studland Bay. In the woodland behind this, an assortment of passerines may be seen and heard, including chaffinches, robins and wrens. We went down onto the beach where, to the right, we could see the chalk stack known as Old Harry's Wife. When we had walked some distance along the beach to the left, we looked back and could see Old Harry himself – a much larger stack and a well-known landmark in the area.

As we walked along the beach, we kept an eye on the water of the bay, and were soon rewarded with the sight of a great crested grebe appearing and disappearing at intervals. As always around this area, cormorants were flying to and fro, together with herring and black-headed gulls. At various times of the year, quite an assortment of birds has been seen in the bay – eiders, scoters, Slavonian and black-necked grebes and red-breasted mergansers in winter, while terns (probably from their nesting sites at nearby Brownsea Island), ringed plovers and oystercatchers are often about. Pied wagtails frequent the shoreline, hunting busily for flies in the seaweed. At migration times, shearwaters, skuas and gannets may be seen off shore.

We also looked for shells, particularly one that occurs only at Studland, Weymouth and the Channel Islands – the rare bivalve, Pandora. On this occasion we found, as always, hundreds of slipper limpets and razors shells, but no Pandoras. The razor shells are probably the remains of the Studland population that was wiped out in the severe 1962/63 winter.

A yellow post at the edge of the dunes marks the start of the sand-dune trail. Turning inland, we climbed up through the fore-dunes, which are held together by sea lyme grass, sand couch and, towards the top, marram grass. Marram, unlike the two former plants, is not resistant to salt. From the top of this first ridge, formed since the last war and known as Zero Ridge, we went down into the valley or dune slack. This area, now covered with gorse, sallow and cross-leaved heath, together with mosses and sundews in the damper parts, was actually part of the beach as recently as 1930. The only birds we saw in this area were meadow pipits.

It was interesting to see, quite plainly, the stages in succession of plants which indicate the change from the marram-covered dunes on the windward side of Zero Ridge, to the dune heathland which takes over on the next ridge. This next ridge is known – logically – as First Ridge, as indeed it was the first ridge of sand-dunes when the area was first surveyed in the 1930s. On this ridge there is much more heather, with bell heather beginning to appear, which is an indication of drier soil. We saw more meadow pipits there. From the top of First Ridge we had a good view of the much wetter slack in between it and the third or Inner Ridge. We also had a good picture of the succession of the dunes.

In the wetter dune slacks there are a number of old bomb craters. The whole area was used during the last war as a rehearsal ground for the Normandy landings and there are still unexploded missiles that surface from time to time. Therefore, any metal object should be left strictly alone and reported to the police. Similarly, on the edge of the beach, small objects that look like water-worn pebbles should not be touched, as a number have turned out to be pieces of phosphorous, which can cause serious burns. The bomb craters are now full of water, providing habitats for water plants and animals. By their margins, fine specimens of the increasingly rare Royal fern are growing. The reserve is also noted for the number of dragon- and damselflies to be seen, particularly over and round this water.

From the top of the Inner Ridge we could see part of the large lake which dominates the reserve. Known as Little Sea, it is about a mile long and is of great ornithological interest. However, we decided to leave that, and the woodland nature trail which we knew would take us to it, until another day, and we returned to the car-park.

The day we chose to do the woodland walk turned out to be one of the worst we have ever endured on a birdwatching expedition as far as the weather was concerned. It blew a gale and poured with rain non-stop. It was the day we proved quite conclusively that our guaranteed waterproof jackets were not! We were absolutely soaked, but in a perverse kind of way we enjoyed it, and finished by congratulating ourselves on sticking it out!

The walk starts in an open, sandy area, but quickly goes into birch woodland with some sallow in the damper parts, where a variety of birds may be seen, depending on the time of year. The resident wrens, blackbirds, robins and chaffinches are commonplace, and during the summer chiffchaffs, redpolls, whitethroats and willow warblers are present. Sparrow-hawks prey on the smaller birds. We saw signs of roe deer, with slot marks and fumets, but did not actually see the animals themselves.

At migration times gannets are just one of the species which may be seen off shore from the Studland Heath Reserve.

We walked past a small pond where, in summer, one might expect to see dragon- and damselflies, and soon came to the edge of Little Sea. It has been formed over about 400 years by the joining of two arms of sand-dunes, so that now it is completely separated from Studland Bay. We entered the hide at the water's edge, but saw few of the 2,000 wildfowl that may be present during the winter months. There were a few tufted ducks and mallard taking shelter in the reeds and little inlets, but the water was rough and the rain absolutely bucketing down – not good weather even for water birds. These two species are joined by wigeons, pintails, shovelers, teal and a few others during the winter; while in the autumn, quite large numbers of Canada geese are seen as they fly across the lake on their way to feed on stubble fields on the nearby Downs. Cormorants we did see, but not herons, which, during the breeding season, often come over from the heronry on Brownsea

Island.

Leaving the hide, we pressed on, coming quite soon to an alder carr, with adjoining swampy ground where, during the summer, reed warblers and buntings are seen. At any time of the year water rails may be heard and possibly seen around the lake's edge. From the lake, we struck back towards the sea and, as we came over one of the sand-dune ridges, we discovered where most of the wildfowl were sheltering. A great array of mallard, teal and wigeons got up from where they had been paddling around among the reeds and rushes in some very swampy ground.

We had, by this time, deserted the formal trail, and walked through part of the well-established heathland where, under different circumstances, we might have seen one of the reserve's rare treasures – a Dartford warbler. All we did see was a couple of bedraggled linnets and some meadow pipits. Nightjars are often present on the heathland in summer. We returned to the car along the beach, soaked, but exhilarated in the strange way that one can be when battling with the elements.

Studland is also well known for other features of wildlife that we did not see on these particular visits. It is remarkable in having all six British reptiles – the rare sand lizard, the common lizard (which we did see), the slow worm, the adder, the grass snake and the rare smooth snake. Botanically too, the reserve is interesting; it is one of the few sites of Dorset heath, and also has a variety of mosses and liverworts, marsh gentian, and water plants such as the greater bladderwort and the very rare small quillwort.

Dawlish Warren
Local Nature Reserve

Managing Body   Teignbridge District Council.
Access   SX 9879. Car-park under railway bridge in Dawlish Warren.
Other information   Guided tours: contact Teignbridge District Council, 0626 66951. Booklet available in local shops.

This reserve on the Exe Estuary achieved national fame when it was the subject of one of the BBC's *Birdwatch* features with Tony Soper. It is a superb place for watching waders and wildfowl, and one of the most enjoyable reserves we have visited – certainly one of the most rewarding. The land is owned partly by Teignbridge District Council and partly by the Devon Trust for Nature Conservation. A hide, financed by the RSPB and the Devon Birdwatching and Preservation Society, is sited at the far end of the Warren

The Exe Estuary is a superb place for watching waders; here a mixed flock takes to the air as the tide comes in.

overlooking a wide, shallow bay which is a marvellous place for viewing the roosting waders at close quarters.

We arrived on a very cold, windy December day, clad in the 'complete gear' of waterproof jackets, trousers, wellingtons, headgear and Balaclavas, and made our way to the shore to walk around the point to the hide. The shore is intersected at intervals by groynes, and the edges of the sand-dunes are protected by stone-filled cages in an attempt to stabilise the mobile dune system and prevent the sea from destroying the Warren. The tide was coming in, but still some way out, and we could see a number of birds on the exposed sandbanks off shore. These proved to be oystercatchers, with one or two cormorants. A little later we saw scoters and eiders flying low over the sea, together with a few wigeons. On the shore itself, we caught up with a sanderling scurrying along just above the waterline.

Climbing up into the sand-dunes, we followed the well-worn tracks around to the bay, where the hide is situated. Even before we reached it, we saw dozens of dark-bellied brent geese out on the mud-flats feeding, presumably, on the eel-grass, two varieties of which grow there. There were also huge flocks of dunlin over the estuary, and on the far side a mixed collection of gulls – herring, black-backed and greater black-backed.

We entered the two-storied hide and looked out over the estuary. The tide was coming in, and we saw an enormous number of waders on the sandbanks. There were hundreds of oystercatchers, making a dramatic and constantly changing black patch on the sand; dunlins were also in abundance; and there were knots, a few shelducks, and, out in the main channel, we could see a great crested grebe. Slavonian grebes are also seen in the area. On the mud-flats, a few curlews were stalking around, and in the pools just in front of the hide several redshanks were busy feeding. We watched, enthralled, as the tide came in, causing the birds to take to the air every so often and settle ever nearer to the hide. As they did so, we picked out a greenshank, some grey plovers, and, both here and further towards the railway embankment, some bar-tailed godwits – one, rather unusually, still in its summer plumage. Several turnstones were running about, as were a few ringed plovers.

During the summer months, in addition to waders, the Warren is a prime place for terns – little and common in fairly large numbers, with Sandwich not unusual, and there may be the occasional Arctic and roseate for the lucky watcher. From August until October there is always a chance of seeing little stints or a curlew sandpiper, while whimbrels may be seen on passage. The avocets, for which the estuary is a well-known area, are more likely to be seen in the upper estuary which is not part of the Dawlish Warren Reserve.

Reluctantly we left the hide to return to the car-park. By now it was blowing a gale, and we struggled along the beach into the driving rain. We simply could not see a thing – but it did not matter – the stay in the hide had been more than worth it!

We paid another visit to Dawlish later on, and took one of the excellent guided tours of the reserve led by the warden. If these are still running, we can recommend them without hesitation, as not only did we see the birds, but the warden was able to point out where some of the 450 species of flowering plants occur, including the Warren crocus, in its only site on mainland Britain. It is also a good area for orchids, with large numbers of the southern marsh orchid in early summer and, later in the year, autumn lady's tresses. He also explained the problem of the garden escape, the tree lupin, which, although it provides a blaze of colour when in flower, must be controlled as it threatens to 'shade out' smaller and less vigorous plants.

We also visited Langstone Rock which, although not on the reserve, is very near it – taking the opposite direction when leaving the car-park. From its heights, it is possible to see far out to sea, and it provides a good view of any ducks or divers which may be about. We saw both red-throated and great northern divers off shore, as well as red-breasted mergansers. Another bird which may be seen in this area is the cirl bunting, which is mainly restricted to the South Devon coastal strip.

One boundary of the reserve runs right alongside the main London to Exeter railway line. It is possible, with due caution, to cross the line at certain points, and obtain another view of the birds in and around the wader roosts, looking across towards the hide. We had excellent views of bar-tailed godwits from there.

For anyone just starting birdwatching, this is a particularly good reserve to visit, because the birds come very close to the hide at high tide, which makes identification so much easier.

Yarner Wood
National Nature Reserve

Managing Body   NCC.
Access   SX 7879. See chapter for details.
Other information   Leaflets available on site or from NCC.

Yarner Wood, on the eastern edge of Dartmoor, is a woodland reserve consisting of an area of about 370 acres lying on steep ground between two small river valleys, rising to some 1,000 feet at the western end. The woodland cover is mostly sessile oak and birch, with some conifer; there is also an area of moorland. It is one of those very pleasant reserves which is not particularly spectacular, but which has many interesting features and a fairly typical list of woodland and moorland birds.

Within the reserve, which was declared a National Nature Reserve in 1952, are two marked trails for which leaflets are available. The longer of the two is a woodland walk of about three and a quarter miles; the shorter, a nature trail of a mile and a half. Access to parts of the reserve away from the trails is by permit only. We decided to follow the shorter of the two walks, partly because it was described in rather more detail in the leaflet, and partly because it is the one followed by the majority of visitors to the reserve.

From the car-park, just off the Bovey Tracey to Manaton road, we started up a small flight of steps and along the path to the first post on the trail, in an area of moorland. As the guide suggested, we looked back the way we had come and saw that the wood was set on the side of a valley, overlooked by moorland, with farm land below. On the left was a conifer woodland, planted in the nineteenth century, consisting of Scots and Corsican pine, with larch and a few sweet chestnuts. A pair of buzzards nest in the wood from time to time, and it so happened that a single bird was soaring high up as we watched. We glimpsed a tree pipit in one of the Scots pines.

We heard but did not see a wood warbler in Yarner – but we did see
and hear plenty of robins.

We continued the trail across the moorland, with its heather and
gorse, watching a number of stonechats as they flitted from bush to
bush, and soon came to the second post on the trail in an area of
encroaching birch wood, with some oaks. Management of this is
taking place to ensure that the birch does not encroach too far, and
controlled burning is carried out to ensure a mixture of moorland
plants and shrubs of varying ages, which offer shelter to a variety of
moorland birds and insects.

From there the trail re-enters Yarner Wood itself through a gap in
a bank that encircles it. As the leaflet points out, boundary banks
like this are common in Devon and are often centuries old. Most of
this part of the wood is oak, but there is a section of young beech
and Japanese larch, planted 1955-77, as its dense foliage helps act as
a shield against fire. In this wood we saw a number of birds –
robins, tits, wrens and a pied flycatcher. Leaving the beech and
maple, we moved on into an area of young birches with an
understorey of bracken and bramble, sheltering robins and wrens.
Throughout the wood we both saw and heard jays and great
spotted woodpeckers. Apparently in winter (we were there in
summer) flocks of siskins feed on the birch seed.

Next to post five of the trail was a large wood ant nest – just one, it seems, of about 800 in the wood. No wonder there were quite a few woodpeckers about! From this point there was a short-cut back to the car-park, but we were enjoying our walk far too much even to think of taking that. We went on into what is the older part of the wood – nearly all oak trees, with an understorey of bilberry, some rowan and plenty of holly – the latter being very popular with redwings and thrushes in winter. The oaks held a selection of small birds – robins, tree-creepers, dozens of tits, nuthatches, and, to our considerable satisfaction we heard a wood warbler. Unfortunately, we could not actually have seen it without leaving the track. The temptation to stray from the path in this wood was considerable at times, but had to be resisted!

The leaflet pointed out an interesting feature of the rowan trees. They are all much the same age, and probably date from the 1950s when the Nature Conservancy Council repaired the fences, so keeping out all the sheep and cattle that previously had access to the wood and had prevented the growth of the young trees.

When we visited the reserve several years ago a section of oaks were part of a study programme concerning their age, and were marked with numbers. I expect these are still there. To demonstrate the ageing process, there was a section of an old tree showing the various parts of the wood and the annual rings. Throughout this trail there are a number of little displays, illustrating various points of interest.

In this area, and at other places within the woodland, we saw a number of nest boxes, most of which are used by tits. A few, however, are used by pied flycatchers – and this represents a notable success for the reserve. These birds were very rare in Devon prior to 1955 when the boxes were first put up, but that year, one pair nested in a box, and in due course the population built up to about twenty in the 1970s, before falling again to about fifteen. However, birds ringed at Yarner Wood have started colonies at other sites in the county. It is an interesting point that some birds return to the same box in Yarner after their winter spent in West Africa.

Our downhill path led us in due course to post eight by a stream; birch and alder were the dominant trees here. The stream is known as Woodcock, and the bird after which it is named visits the wood in winter, feeding on the worms in the soft, wet soil. It is a remarkable bird – its eyes set high and well back on the head, so that it can see all round when it is probing for food with its long and very sensitive bill. Its well-known 'roding' display flight, when it flies around the boundaries of its territory, uttering its guttural croaking call, is one of the unusual sights and sounds of ornithology.

55

The steady, purposeful flight of roding is such a contrast to the quick, dodging dash for cover it makes when disturbed on the ground. The male woodcock is polygamous; having successfully attracted a female by his flight he will mate, then set off again and repeat the process with another female. The frequently mentioned behaviour of the female in moving her young to a place of safety by taking to the air with one held between her thighs or in her claws is, alas, more often spoken or written about than seen.

Some of the trees in the vicinity of post nine on the trail are of interest from an unnatural, as distinct from a natural history point of view. In 1942 an incendiary bomb started a large fire in the wood, and the scars from this can be seen to this day on the trunks of some of the larger trees. Many of the young trees at the time were killed. Shoots grew from the stumps of these trees, giving a coppiced effect, which is probably just how it looked in medieval times, when coppicing was practised and the poles used for charcoal making. There are the remains of a number of old charcoal hearths throughout the wood.

We turned left at a junction of several rides, and, after a short walk, found ourselves standing in what is described in the guide as the dry bed of the Bovey Tracey Pottery Leat – a leat being the local term for an artificial water channel. This one dates from about the middle of the last century and carried water to a pottery in Bovey Tracey. From a naturalist's point of view it is most noteworthy for the number of mosses which grow along its banks. A little further along, the dry bed has been made into a ride, and the guide points out how past management has influenced the oaks that grow on each side. Those on the valley side above the ride are small and crooked, an indication of former coppicing, while the trees on the other side are much taller and straighter, and were probably left to provide larger timber. In this area, as in so much of Yarner Wood, tits, tree-creepers, robins and nuthatches were the principal birds to be seen.

From here, the trail led past some big old beech trees and finally back across the stream to the car-park – after a very enjoyable walk through a delightful woodland reserve.

Because of the necessity to remain on the paths, we did not see everything in the wood, and had to rely on the NCC leaflet to learn more of the management that is going on in it. The principal aim is to diversify the trees and to encourage the woodland to become self-generating. In the 1950s, the leaflet told us, small plots in the reserve were clear-felled and replanted with a mixture of oak, ash, wych elm, alder, Scots pine and hazel – all native trees which might have been there in primeval times. Large scale thinning has been carried out in certain areas to encourage natural regeneration, and the whole aim is to encourage a diversity not only of tree species, but of all kinds of wildlife, including birds.

In addition to the birds and plants already mentioned, the reserve also offers habitats for red, fallow and roe deer. There are several badger setts, while the ponds hold palmate newts, frogs and toads. Dormice are not uncommon and frequently use the nest boxes provided for the birds.

Braunton Burrows and the Taw/Torridge Estuary

Managing body   NCC.
Access   SS 4633. See chapter for details.
Other information   Leaflet available at newsagents in Braunton or from NCC. No access to certain areas when flags flying – military exercises in progress. Warden: Braunton 812552.

Braunton Burrows is a National Nature Reserve consisting of a huge area of sand-dunes (the largest dune system in Britain) extending over nearly 1,500 acres, and abutting, in the south, onto the estuaries of the Taw and Torridge rivers in North Devon. It is a fascinating place – not just for the birdwatcher, but especially for the botanist. The Burrows are very colourful at certain times of the year, with a mass of wild flowers. The estuary itself is not really part of the reserve, but as that is where the majority of the birds can be seen and as the boundaries of one are close to the other, I am going to include it.

The Burrows are open to the public at almost all times, but on some occasions military exercises take place over an area leased to the Ministry of Defence, and access may be restricted. There are two free car-parks; one approached from the B3231 Braunton to Saunton road, and the other may be reached by continuing past this car-park along a diabolical track – the American Road (the Americans rehearsed their Normandy landings here) – and people with respect for their cars would do better to pay the small toll on the toll-road from Broadsands!

The dune system makes a very interesting study. It consists of a series of ridges up to 100 feet high, separated by slacks and intersected by cross ridges and dune blow-outs. The dunes have been built up by sand from the beach being blown up against grass and collecting there. As the marram grows up through the sand (up to a metre a year has been recorded) more sand collects, and so it goes on. Once the sand has become stable, the growth of marram declines and other plants are able to colonise, and thus a botanical variety is built up. It is important, however, that the plant cover is preserved from excessive trampling. Measures have to be taken to protect some of the most popular areas – an example of this is the wooden boardwalk which leads from the car-park at Broadsands to the shore at Crow Beach.

In an effort to increase the habitats, the NCC has dug a number of ponds throughout the Burrows. There are also a number of dune slacks which flood during the winter, although they dry out during the summer. It was very dry when we were there, so we saw no open water at all, but we could see where it had been. We also saw some of the dried out slacks, where, in early summer, marsh marigolds flower, followed later on by marsh orchids and marsh helleborines. We did see some round-leaved wintergreen which was first found on the reserve in 1958 and is now quite common.

Among the fixed dunes there were huge areas of the lovely pale yellow evening primrose, and on the sides of some of the dunes we found patches of sand pansies. In other parts, viper's bugloss was growing in profusion, with its spectacular vivid blue flowers. Short-eared owls, merlins and harriers hunt the dunes in migration times, but we saw nothing more exciting than a kestrel – plus some magpies and crows.

After wandering around near the Sandy Lane car-park, we took the American Road down to the southern end of the reserve and walked down to the shore. A number of birds were out on the water – ducks in eclipse for the most part, and not easy to identify at a distance. We spent an enjoyable time examining the patches of glasswort growing on the mud-flats, before returning and taking the boardwalk to Crow Beach. This took us through the dunes, where we saw a number of small birds, such as wheatears, stonechats and linnets. We decided to leave further examination of the flora until the return journey, as we wanted to reach the beach before the tide came in too far.

At the beach, we saw a number of waders typical of the estuary – oystercatchers, curlews and dunlins. The area is known to be rich in birds, with the list including the ringed plover, golden plover, lapwing, ruff, grey plover, greenshank, redshank, spotted redshank, turnstone and sanderling – in other words, most of the waders to be seen in many an estuary around our shores. Wildfowl are to be seen too – wigeons, shelducks, mallard, teal, tufted ducks, shovelers and goldeneyes. The estuary is on the west coast migration route and huge flocks of birds congregate at these times, with many passage migrants using the reserve for roosting and feeding.

On the return journey, we paid more attention to the plants,

A curlew – a typical estuarine bird seen at Braunton Burrows.
Its bill (longer in the female than the male) is ideally adapted
for mud-flat feeding.

finding many examples of prickly saltwort and sea rocket just above
the strand line at the foot of the dunes. Among the marram of the
fore-dunes we found some plants of the rare sea stock – and a bit of
searching produced one in flower, which was exciting. There were
tamarisk trees growing a little further back, and a great variety of
mosses in the dune slacks. Wild thyme was growing in scented
patches. In some of the damper patches, the curious horse-tails
were growing. Whenever I see one of these relatively primitive and
now quite small plants, I am reminded that their ancestors – some
of which stood nearly one hundred feet high – were one of the
dominant features of Britain's vegetation 350 million or so years
ago, in the days when dinosaurs roamed the countryside.

The reserve is noted for butterflies such as dark green fritillaries,
marbled whites and, in late summer, huge clouds of meadow
browns and gatekeepers.

We thoroughly enjoyed Braunton Burrows, although we did not
see a great variety or number of birds there. It is a delightful place –
one we would like to visit again, possibly in winter or spring.

The Tamar Estuary

Managing body   Cornwall Trust for Nature Conservation.
Access   SX 4362 (Cargreen village), SX 4461 (Landulph), SX 4262
(Botusfleming and Moditonham Quay). Lanes off A388 from Saltash –
Callington road.

The Tamar Estuary contains the most extensive area of mud-flats
and salt marsh in the south-west of England. It is a marvellous place
for birds, especially in winter and at migration times. There are
three particularly good vantage points around the estuary on the
Cornish side; these are managed by the Cornish Naturalists' Trust.

We went in winter, and our first stop was in the little village of
Landulph, where we parked by the church and walked down the
lane and across the fields to the sea-wall which borders the estuary.
We approached the wall and peered over cautiously, to avoid
disturbing the birds we could hear calling. It was very foggy, and, as
we looked over, although we could hear the birds we could not see
much – we could not even see the massive Tamar Bridge through
the murk.

We climbed over the wall and dropped down onto the shaly
shingle of the shore, hoping that the fog would clear before the tide
came in and the birds moved off elsewhere. We were lucky – it did
– and spread out in front of us was a great apron of mud-flats, with
dozens of birds dotted all over it, and more on the water of the
deep channels out in the middle. Soon we could see the bridge and
the opposite shore of the small arm of the estuary where we were
standing.

Most of the waders we could see were curlews and redshanks,
with a few dunlins and one or two bar-tailed godwits. Other
species are often seen here, and these include the greenshank,
spotted redshank, knot and whimbrel. There were also many
shelducks plodding about and cormorants going to and fro. The
ducks on the channel were not easy to identify as the fog was still
hanging over the water, but from their size we thought they were
mallard and some wigeons. As we watched, the tide began to come
in quite rapidly, and the birds moved with it. Within just half an
hour the mud-flats were covered and the birds had moved right
upstream, probably to Kingsmill Lake.

The following day we went to the next vantage point at
Moditonham Quay. It was brought home to us quite forcibly here
that, while travelling in a fairly bulky motor caravan has lots of
advantages in terms of comfort and facilities, it also has distinct

Moditonham Quay – a peaceful, remote, and utterly lovely place on
the Tamar Estuary.

disadvantages, such as lack of manoeuvrability in narrow Cornish
lanes! We followed the lane down to Moditonham Quay, and
found, on arrival, that there was nowhere to park and very little
space in which to turn. Eventually, we did manage to turn and
backed into the approach road to the quay – a space that would
have been snug for a Mini. There was no question of getting out of
the driver's or passenger's doors – the back door was the only one
we could open. However, having negotiated all that, we found it
was a very special place indeed – a secluded arm of the estuary with
steeply sloping fields and woods going down to the water's edge.
The tide was right out, exposing mud-flats which were dotted with
waders. As we walked to the edge of the quay, a curlew got up and
flew off, uttering its wild, bubbling call, which seemed to echo
round the hills surrounding this peaceful, remote and lovely place.
A few herons stood impassively round the margins of the inlet, and
as we climbed down onto the mud-flats, one took off and flew
ponderously upstream and out of sight.

The only thing that was not so lovely about Moditonham was the
mud – grey, smelly and glutinous – but clearly the birds relished it.
As we rounded a bend another little inlet lay before us, where
dozens of redshanks were feeding. The ones nearest to us bobbed
their heads a little anxiously as we appeared, but we stood quietly
and they soon continued their probing. A few snipe were also busy
in the rough grass along the far side of the inlet. After watching for

some time, we returned to the quay and sat there, looking across to a sloping field on the far side. We soon realised that, as the evening was closing in, more and more birds were coming to roost there. Most were lapwings, with the occasional curlew and redshank – no doubt arriving from other parts of the estuary as the tide came in.

The next day, we set off to the third of the viewing points at Cargreen village, further up the Tamar. It was here that we hoped to see at least some of the flock of avocets that spend every winter on the estuary. Cargreen is a delightful place, the main street leading right down to the river, where it looks across quite a wide stretch of water to Devon. It is a popular place for the boating fraternity, with plenty of craft of all kinds, which one might have thought would disturb the birds, but did not seem to.

As we arrived at the sea-wall a great flock of dunlins took to the air on the far shore. It is a sight we never tire of seeing – and we watched with considerable pleasure as they wheeled, flashing first grey, then white in the brilliant sunshine.

We were told that a flock of avocets had just been seen at Cargreen and had flown off downstream. We decided, however, to make our way further upstream along a pathway that led along the shore. As soon as we were away from the built-up area we saw plenty of curlews, redshanks and shelducks feeding on the mud-flats and sandbanks. Other people we met during our walk spoke of having seen the avocets. They had 'just been' practically everywhere! It was very frustrating, as we had not seen a sign of them.

As we walked on, the views across the river were lovely, and there were plenty of other birds to watch, with more dunlins moving about on the far shore. After a time, we came to the end of the path along the shore-line so we struck off inland along a footpath that took us high above the estuary, through farmland. Mixed flocks of finches flew from bush to bush in front of us and into some reed-beds on the side of the path – gold- and greenfinches mostly. In the wetlands near the reed-beds a number of snipe got up and winged rapidly away as we approached, and a kestrel hovered overhead.

We walked and walked, revelling in the beauty of the day and the scenery – but still saw no avocets. Eventually we could go no further and turned back. And, just as we turned, there they were – two groups of black and white birds. The chevrons on their wings were clearly visible, as seven or eight of them flew low over the water, followed by a single bird. At last we had seen them! It was a tremendous thrill. We rushed to the headland to follow their progress, and they came down on what appeared to be a sandbank some distance from the shore, and then took to the water in a very shallow channel, swimming along, sweeping their elegant curved bills from side to side as they searched for food. It was a sight well worth waiting for, and as they finally sailed out of view, we made our way back to the village, pausing from time to time to see if we could glimpse them again.

It is pleasing that these graceful birds can now be seen in an increasing number of places, and how grateful we all must be for the marvellous work done by the RSPB, which has succeeded, first at Havergate and then at Minsmere, in encouraging the return of the avocets as a breeding species after an absence of over 100 years. The colony at Havergate now numbers about 100 pairs, and there are more than 50 at Minsmere – a most heartening success story.

Having finally seen the avocets we returned to the car well content with our day's 'birding'.

Stithians Reservoir

Managing Body   Cornwall Birdwatching and Preservation Society.
Access   SW 7136. Take B3297 south from Redruth (see chapter for details).
Other information   Permit to enter reserve from South-west Water Authority, Barnfield Lane, Exeter. Key to hide from Cornwall Birdwatching and Preservation Society, 0840 213415.

Stithians Reservoir is an ideal place for disabled birdwatchers, as so much of what is to be seen can be viewed from a car. The best approach is via the B3297 road from Redruth to Four Lanes, then a minor road to Penhalvean and follow the signs. The road crosses one end of the reservoir at a very narrow point by means of a causeway. If there is not too much traffic about, it is possible to stop on or very close to the causeway itself and look down onto the water on either side.

In a sheltered stretch of water to the right of the road we saw dozens of ducks – pochards, tufteds, goldeneyes and mallard, with a few wigeons. As we watched, a huge flock of golden plovers alighted on a field sloping away from the water, where we had a really good view of them. There were a few herons around the pool's edge and also some waders – redshanks and curlews. Some remarkable rarities have been recorded at Stithians – blue-winged teal, ring-necked ducks and lesser yellow-legs.

Moving on to the far shore of the reservoir, we saw the Cornwall Birdwatching and Preservation Society's hide, and had the good fortune to meet a member, who kindly allowed us to use it while he was there. There were dozens of wigeons close in shore, and, on a small promontory, an astonishing number of herons – in a very small area we counted about fifteen.

A permit is normally necessary to enter the fenced-off areas of the reserve, but there is plenty to see without those.

Hayle Estuary

Managing body   RSPB.
Access   SW 5537 Take St Ives turning off A30 Hayle – Penzance road. Old Quay House Inn immediately on right with car-park.
Other information   RSPB hide in garden. Information centre near hide.

Hayle Estuary is not a reserve as such. It is, however, a good place for seeing birds; there is an excellent RSPB hide and information centre, and formal bird reserves are a bit thin on the ground in this part of Cornwall – although there are many places where birds may be seen.

This is another unusual site, as the main A30 Hayle to Penzance road runs along one side of it, but the constant traffic does not seem to disturb the birds in the least. It is a notable place for rare sightings, with records of American wigeons, long-billed dowitchers and white-rumped sandpipers.

As with all estuaries, the best birdwatching at Hayle is during the two hours either side of high tide, but, because of the comparative narrowness of the estuary and the proximity of the birds to the various vantage points, something of interest may be seen at virtually any time of the day. We spent an absorbing couple of hours in the hide, watching at really close quarters as a variety of waders picked around the mud-flats. There were plenty of redshanks, dunlins, curlews and oystercatchers, a few turnstones, godwits and ringed plovers, and huge flocks of lapwings which 'commute' between the estuary and the low-lying fields just the other side of the main road. At any time they may be put up by a peregrine or a sparrow-hawk.

A large number of golden plovers often roost on the estuary during the winter, as do knots, but we saw no sign of them. One or two herons were standing on the water's edge or stalking along the banks. In the various deep channels that run through the estuary, we saw a number of ducks, including a female goosander, while shelducks were out in the centre of the mud-flats. Little grebes popped up and down the main channel. Teal, goldeneyes and red-breasted mergansers may also be seen.

After visiting the excellent RSPB centre, we walked back along

Huge flocks of lapwings 'commute' between the estuary and the low-lying fields just the other side of the main road.

the A30 beside the sea-wall towards Hayle town. We had more good views of waders, and after about half a mile we clambered over the wall and down onto the rocky shore. From there we had access to the footpath running across a high embankment which encloses the non-tidal Carnsew Pool. In the pool, we had very close views of several great crested grebes – so close that we could see them swimming under water very clearly.

We were also delighted to find two great northern divers and were able to watch them diving for fish and flying from one end of the pool to the other. They are by no means uncommon visitors to Hayle; most of the birds seen here originating from Iceland. The great northern is the largest of the three divers seen in Britain and, although not recognised as a breeding species here, one pair was seen with young on a Scottish loch in 1970, and there are other reports which suggest that this handsome bird may be extending its range. Apart from its larger size, the great northern diver may be distinguished from the black- and red-throated species by its markedly hunched position in the water and its thicker neck. The eerie call of this lovely bird evokes thoughts of remote and magical Highland lochs.

In the summer, the visitor might do well to take the road to Lelant near St Ives, and walk across to the Port Kidney sands ternery. Hayle Estuary is easily accessible and rewarding, and repays a visit at almost any time of the year.

Central England

Earl's Hill Nature Reserve

Managing body   Shropshire Trust for Nature Conservation.
Access   SJ 4105. Park behind Alexander & Duncan's garage on A488 at Pontesbury village, 7 miles south-west of Shrewsbury. Follow lane south to where reserve is signposted.
Other information   Visitor centre open every summer weekend. Nature trail guide from Trust, visitor centre or garage.

Earl's Hill Reserve, the first opened by the Shropshire Trust for Nature Conservation, is not primarily a bird reserve, but its wooded and grassy slopes, its damp valleys and its stream offer varied habitats for a range of woodland birds. It also has an impressive selection of butterflies, as well as interesting plants.

Two leaflets are available, either from the Trust office in Shrewsbury, from the reserve centre which is open on most summer weekends or from the forecourt of Alexander and Duncan's garage on the corner of the A488 road and the lane which leads to the reserve. One leaflet gives a general description of the reserve together with a helpful profile of Earl's Hill; the other is a more detailed guide to the nature trail.

We parked behind the garage and walked half a mile or so up to the track leading into the reserve. The rutted track skirted the edge of the steep and heavily wooded hill before emerging into a field, where a signpost pointed down the hill to the visitor centre and up the hill to the reserve. As the centre was not open we headed straight for the reserve. From the entrance gate we had a good view of the hill which rises dramatically more than 1,000 feet above the surrounding Shropshire Plain. The outstanding feature was an almost sheer rock-face consisting of some of the oldest rock in Britain, dating back more than 1,200 million years.

Several jackdaws were performing aerial acrobatics off the cliff-face, while above them a kestrel hovered before dropping dramatically out of sight behind the hill. Ravens are sometimes seen around the crags.

A little further on we came to a section of scree at the foot of the crag. There appeared to have been a fairly recent rock-fall, as the plants we expected to see at this particular point were missing. According to the leaflet, many of the stones should have been covered with mosses and lichens, and, in the humus between the rocks, the rare yellow stonewort and the wall pennywort should have been growing. However, the only signs we saw were the leaves of the pennywort at the edges of the scree. Young ash trees, recently established were also growing there.

The next stopping place on the trail was a grassy bank which merged into scrubland, where we heard at least one and probably two grasshopper warblers. Tree pipits were also in evidence around this area. We saw a number of butterflies, including small tortoiseshells, gatekeepers and peacocks. Others recorded on that section of the reserve include red admirals, commas and small coppers. A sudden commotion in the scrub startled us momentarily, until a rather dishevelled sheep emerged – one of a number on the reserve that help to control the invasion of the scrub into the open grassland.

Moving on, we had a choice of following the trail down into the valley or of going up the hill towards the summit. Hot though it was, we opted for the latter, deciding that it would be a pleasant end to the day to descend from the hot heights into the cool valley.

The path continued diagonally up and around the hill to the summit – quite a stiff climb. It was worth it, however, because although we did not see much in the way of bird-life other than a solitary buzzard, the view of the North Shropshire Plain to the north and Long Mynd to the south was tremendous. Included in the trail leaflet was a circular dial, which can be placed on the Ordnance Survey triangulation pillar, and lined up so as to identify points of interest in the surrounding countryside.

From the summit we re-traced our steps to where the trail divided, and plunged down the hill through fairly dense bracken into the wood which consisted initially of oak with a number of dead elms. We heard the yaffle of a green woodpecker and saw some black and white woodpeckers, one of which was scurrying up the trunk of a dead elm in search of insects.

There were some nest boxes among the trees, and although it was quite late in the summer, a number of pied flycatchers were still flitting about, no doubt having raised their broods in the boxes. The provision of the boxes has, it appears, greatly encouraged the species to spread beyond its rather limited British range, and has also done much to overcome the problems caused by forest clearance.

The breeding plumage of the male pied flycatcher is unmistakable – with its black back, white forehead and white wing patches and underparts. The white breast is displayed prominently during courtship. The birds arrive in April and May from Africa, and the male immediately sets about finding a suitable nesting hole – often ones previously occupied by woodpeckers. The more soberly-plumaged female does the bulk of the nest building, using bark, honeysuckle if available, and grass for lining. Up to six pale blue eggs are laid, and incubated for twelve to thirteen days by the female; the young are then fed by both parents. Although the birds do indulge in typical flycatcher behaviour catching insects on the wing when necessary, they frequently abandon this in favour of feeding on caterpillars found among oak foliage.

Other trees in the wood included ash and some wych elm, and throughout we saw tits, tree-creepers and one or two nuthatches. At the bottom of quite a steep path, some of which was cut into steps, we came to the very attractive brook, where dippers have been seen. The brook contains mayfly and stonefly nymphs, freshwater shrimps, bullheads and trout. The surrounding area was rich in mosses, lichens and liverworts, while alder trees grew along the banks.

After following the brook for some little way, we climbed up to a stile leading out of the deep wood and into a rough, scrubby area, where we heard a willow warbler. There were a few large ant hills on which, according to the guide, grew various plants, such as

Nuthatches were just one of the woodland birds we saw at Earl's Hill; others included pied flycatchers, tree-creepers, and spotted woodpeckers.

heath bedstraw, thyme, heath speedwell and mouse-ear chickweed.

It had been a pleasant, if rather hot, day. Although we did not see anything of outstanding interest, Earl's Hill is a most attractive reserve, and, on a clear day, the views from the summit are really superb.

Minsmere RSPB Reserve

Managing body RSPB.

Access TM 4768 (NT car-park). From Westleton follow signs to Dunwich. After 1¾ miles turn right at sign to Dunwich Heath and Minsmere. Follow road to NT hut. TM 4767 (reserve). East of East Bridge, reached from B1122 Leiston – Yoxford road. Signpost after leaving East Bridge.

Other information Public hides (always open) reached from NT car-park. Information centre. Trails at reserve. Permits required (sometimes in short supply). Some hides suitable for disabled visitors. Leaflet.

If there is an RSPB 'showpiece' reserve, I suppose it would have to be Minsmere. It is widely known, not just to dedicated ornithologists but to the public at large, and its popularity is underlined by the fact that permits to visit it are sometimes restricted to just half a day per person. With a build-up like that, it might be feared that the reserve would not live up to its reputation, but we found it entirely enthralling, and it is another on the list to be re-visited.

Before visiting Minsmere Reserve itself, we went to the National Trust car-park on Minsmere Cliffs, off the Westleton to Dunwich road. The car-park is situated at the edge of a large area of heathland where, during the summer, nightjars, woodcocks, stonechats, tree and meadow pipits and owls may be seen. A constant procession of sea-birds was moving along the coast, mostly gulls when we were there in winter. Others recorded include auks (much less common in this area) terns and skuas.

From the car-park we walked along behind the high bank screening the reserve, to the first of two splendid public hides, which are open at all times. From here we had magnificent views over the most famous of Minsmere's features – The Scrape – an area of nearly 50 acres of what was originally very unproductive and poor quality reed-bed and couch grass in marshy ground. By much hard work, this area was transformed into a stretch of mud and shallow brackish water of varying depths, with gravel islands, and it now offers rich feeding and good nesting sites for 1,000 or more pairs of birds of over 20 species. In addition, there is excellent viewing, not just from the hides within the reserve, but from the two public ones we were visiting. If any visitor is unlucky enough to reach Minsmere during the height of the summer season when permits are at a premium, then all is not lost – at least The Scrape can be seen from outside the reserve.

Having obtained the necessary permits for Minsmere Reserve from the visitor centre, we had a quick look at the displays in the adjacent information centre before setting off on one of the two well-constructed paths around the reserve, which take in no fewer than nine hides. Three of these, in addition to the two public ones, overlook The Scrape. From these we saw a great variety of birds – nearly all wildfowl – plus dozens of snipe and lapwings, a lone grey plover and plenty of dunlins. The wildfowl included mallard, teal, garganeys, gadwalls, wigeons, shovelers, tufted ducks, with several Canada and greylag geese and a few mute swans. We missed a Slavonian grebe that had been spotted from the West Hide, but we did see a flight of three spotted redshanks heading away from us across the reserve. The list of waders recorded at Minsmere is extensive and among the forty-six listed are the ringed and little ringed plovers, golden plover, curlew, whimbrel, both godwits, greenshank, knot, little and Temminck's stints, sanderling and ruff.

During the summer up to 500 pairs of terns nest, mainly Sandwich and common, with a few pairs of little terns some years. But the great success story of Minsmere is the avocet. It was here that the first four pairs bred in 1947, after an absence from Britain of more than 100 years. This was then followed by a gap of 16 years until 1963 when a single pair raised one chick. Since then, careful management has ensured their continued presence, and in 1981 58 pairs nested.

The reed-beds surrounding the marsh and The Scrape, which extend over a large area of the reserve, are a wonderful habitat for the birds. Bitterns are a breeding species there, and it is apparently not uncommon for one of these remarkable birds to be seen flying over the car-park by the visitor centre. Water rails are always present, while in summer reed and sedge warblers and grasshopper warblers nest in appreciable numbers.

The red walk that we were following led away from The Scrape, through the reed-beds and woodland and via the Treetop Hide to Island Mere Hide, which was especially rewarding. A female marsh harrier was sitting in full view on a post a little distance away, and we were able to see her yellowish head and dark eye-stripe very plainly. After a time, she took off, flapped slowly along just above the reed-bed and settled in a tree. We were fortunate to see several of these striking birds during our visit – all females – but there is some concern that only one or two pairs breed each year.

70

While watching the harrier we heard the distinctive 'clinking' sound of bearded tits and, sure enough, a little party of these delightful birds flitted through the reeds – one or two pausing long enough for us to see them clearly. These, too, are a success story for Minsmere. Less than ten individual birds were known in Britain in 1947; now an average of fifty pairs breed on Minsmere alone.

There are large tracts of woodland on the reserve, about 600 acres altogether. Most are mixed oak, sycamore, beech, birch and Scots pine. A great variety of woodland birds has been recorded – all the tits (except the crested), tawny and occasionally long-eared owls, the three woodpeckers, warblers and the increasingly rare nightingale.

There are also some patches of rhododendrons where a flock of siskins had been seen. We went to look, and sure enough, there they were – one of the few occasions when birds have actually stayed around for us to see them after being told of their presence! In the same scrubland there were also flocks of finches, chiefly green- and goldfinches, and some linnets.

From the rhododendron walk we returned to the car-park passing, on our way, another tree-top hide from which many woodland species may be seen. We had a marvellous day, seeing forty-three species, and although we would have returned the following day had the reserve been open, we decided to do the next best thing and re-visit the public hides.

The first four pairs of avocets bred at Minsmere in 1947, after an absence from Britain of over 100 years.

It turned out to be a good decision, because, as we settled down to watch the wildfowl, we saw a male hen harrier quartering the ground beyond the reed-beds and the scrub. We watched it for some time, and then, to the consternation of the smaller birds, including the dunlins who took off in a great hurry, it flew right across The Scrape in front of the hide and off towards the woodland. After hawking around there for a short time, it returned, and came even closer to the hide. We had a superb view of it, with its striking grey wings with their black tips and trailing edges – so different from the female's dark brown colouring. The grey of this particular male was so pale that the white rump was hardly noticeable. It was a wonderful climax to a delightful few days around Minsmere.

Snettisham RSPB Reserve

Managing body   RSPB.
Access   TF 6533. Beach is signposted from A149 King's Lynn – Hunstanton road in Snettisham village.
Other information   Car-park. Leaflet from reserve or RSPB. Warden: School House, Wolferton, King's Lynn.

Snettisham is an excellent reserve. It covers 3,250 acres on the eastern side of The Wash, and includes vast inter-tidal sands and mud-flats, a shingle beach, flooded gravel pits and a salt marsh. For us, it will always be associated with the quite magical sound of pink-footed geese – skein after skein of them – flying overhead, and calling to each other as they moved from their roosts in the fields behind high banks to their feeding grounds further along the coast. We heard them at first light and again at dusk, chattering among themselves as they settled down for the night. At times, 8,000 or more have been recorded at Snettisham.

At first sight, Snettisham does not look particularly promising for birds, with a large caravan site and a straggling chalet village stretching a mile or so along the coast behind the sea-wall.But first impressions are misleading; it proves to be one of the great birdwatching places in the country.

We walked down to the shore in front of the chalets and, looking along to the left, we could just make out one of the hides in the distance, so off we went. About a quarter of a mile along the shore, we began to see birds on the sand – redshanks mostly, and then, as we approached more closely, the whole expanse of uncovered sand was alive with waders, shelducks and mallard. There were curlews and dunlins, knots and sanderlings, oystercatchers and turnstones and, away in the distance, we could see some brent geese. Every so often a great cloud of dunlins went sweeping along the coastline, and out towards the brents we could also see a huge black mass – thousands of oystercatchers. Just in front of us, ringed plovers were running about on the sand and among the seaweed. Further along, the sand gave way to mud, and although the numbers of birds decreased a little, there were still plenty about. We watched a number of shelducks clambering in and out of a deep channel which wound its way through the flats. A few grey plovers were standing motionless on the mud.

Peak numbers of birds at Snettisham are phenomenal – with totals in the region of 70,000 – 10,000 dunlins, 4,000 bar-tailed godwits, 35,000 knots, 1,500 grey plovers, 1,000 turnstones, 800 sanderlings, 250 ringed plovers, 3,500 redshanks, 13,000 oystercatchers and 1,500 curlews. The wildfowl may total 12,000, with 8,000 pink-foots, 2,000 shelducks, 1,400 brents and 1,000 mallard.

The first hide overlooks one of the flooded gravel pits, which are an important feature of the reserve. Not only are there considerable numbers of wildfowl on these pits, they also act as roosts for many thousands of waders – up to 15,000 – during the winter spring tides. On the pits we saw pochards, mallard, teal, goldeneyes, wigeons, scaups, tufted ducks, great crested, little and black-necked grebes, shovelers and red-breasted mergansers. Other species regularly seen there include the gadwall, smew, and long-tailed duck, and both Bewick's and whooper swans. We did see some whoopers a long way across the fields, but they were not on the reserve. Coots winter on the pits by the dozen. In the summer, up to about 150 pairs of common terns nest on the gravel islands, as well as many gulls.

We visited the other two hides overlooking the pits before returning along the sea-wall. That was rewarding, as we spotted an Arctic skua making its way along the coast, its two long centre tail-feathers making it instantly recognisable. A bird of bullying, piratical habits, it forces other birds such as kittiwakes, gulls and terns to disgorge their prey by swooping on them. During the breeding season, it robs nests of both eggs and young.

The following morning there was a thick fog, but nothing daunted, we set off again along the beach towards the salt marsh. Although we could hear the birds out on the sands, we could see little. Then, a small flock of birds came flitting out of the murk and settled on the grass about twenty yards ahead of us. A quick glance was enough to see that they were a party of snow buntings, their plumage varied as usual. For a while they kept us company, getting up and flying a little way ahead, then settling before flying on again.

73

An Arctic skua – a bird of bullying, piratical habits, and a robber of eggs and nestlings.

Eventually they tired of this and disappeared into the fog.

We looked at the salt marsh, but the middle of winter is not the best time for this particular habitat. In summer it would be much more interesting, with typical plants such as sea aster, sea purslane, sea arrowgrass and stock sea lavender, as well as glasswort and common cordgrass. The shingle too, at the right time of year has good examples of sea sandwort, yellow horned poppy, rocket, seakale, curled dock, hound's tongue and shrubby seablite.

Although it is not part of the reserve, we walked along the beach to the right of the Snettisham car-park, where we saw more waders out on the sands. We then struck inland among the fixed dunes and dune slack, coming eventually to a waterway, which was frozen over. We were very much entertained by the antics of the coots and moorhens that were finding the icy surface extremely difficult to manage.

Snettisham is a superb reserve. Much work has clearly gone into making it such a sanctuary for birds. The provision of screening banks and fences to protect the birds from disturbance caused by people in a very popular tourist area is important. Islands in the gravel pits were constructed to encourage the breeding terns, ducks and waders; and, of course, there are the excellent hides which allow us all to see the wealth of bird-life of this stretch of the coast.

Titchwell Marsh RSPB Reserve

Managing body RSPB.
Access TF 7544. Entrance off A149, half-way between Thornham and Titchwell.
Other information Access at all times. Car-park. Picnic area. Information centre. Leaflet.

There are some reserves which, for no clearly definable reason, hold a special attraction, not just because of the wealth of bird-life, but perhaps for the atmosphere of well-being, caring and enthusiasm that seem to permeate them. Such a one, in our experience, is the RSPB reserve at Titchwell Marsh in Norfolk.

We went first to the visitor centre, which contains a very helpful range of displays explaining how the different habitats on the reserve function. There was also a board with a list of birds seen that day. In addition to the customary RSPB leaflet explaining all about the reserve, we bought a substantial report entitled *Titchwell Marsh – the first ten years*. This contains an enormous amount of information, and is written with obvious enjoyment and enthusiasm.

From the centre, we took the pathway leading down the west of the reserve, from which most of it can be seen and from which access to the main hides is gained. The first of the habitats through which we passed was the reed-beds. Most of the habitats were non-existent before 1963, having been used during the previous 170 years for the production of root crops and beef. In 1953, however, a huge tidal surge breached the sea-wall which protected these activities. In the 30 or so years since then, the land has gradually become salt marsh again, with the resurgence of adjacent and complementary habitats.

The reed-beds, the bulk of which have grown up since 1953, are now both fresh water and tidal, offering food, shelter and nesting sites for reed warblers and buntings. Both of these, together with the bearded tits, nest among the reeds, while bitterns, water rails, harriers, moorhens and mallard nest on the ground in the fresh water areas.

The next habitat we came to was the thirty acres of fresh water marsh, part of a former aster marsh which is now flooded, except

A reed bunting, which with reed warblers and bearded tits, nests in the reed-beds at Titchwell.

for some small islands. This area is managed to keep the water at suitable levels for the changing demands of the wildlife throughout the year. In spring and summer, for example, the level is kept high so as to maintain standing water for the reed-beds. In autumn, the level is reduced to expose the mud for feeding waders, while in winter, it is kept at an intermediate level, so that frosts do not kill the invertebrates in the top few centimetres of mud, which provide food for the birds.

When we were there, various wildfowl and waders were present – teal, wigeons, cormorants, shovelers, snipe and dunlins. Later in the winter, we might have seen Bewick's swans; while in spring garganeys and pintails pass through, as well as black terns and a wide variety of occasional visitors, such as spoonbills, ospreys, glossy ibis and white-winged black terns. Other waders likely to be seen are ruffs, both phalaropes, white-rumped sandpipers and Kentish plovers.

We watched with interest as one of the herons caught and then devoured a very large eel. We doubted that the bird would manage to cram it all in. But it did, and then stood and thought about it for quite some time, looking distinctly bloated around the neck.

A bank divides the main reserve from a former lavender marsh.

Here we had an excellent view of a kestrel on the ground, and also a single grey plover – very conspicuous in its breeding plumage, even at this late date.

The next hide overlooked the boundary between the fresh water and the brackish marsh – an area of about forty acres, twenty-five of which is particularly attractive to birds. It is kept flooded for most of the year, and the open area of mud-flats and shallow water provides habitats suitable for the larvae of flies and, in the deeper water, prawns, gobies, shore crabs and sticklebacks.

There was an interesting variety of birds in this section – notably black-tailed godwits (of which there were quite a number), a few avocets, dunlins, some brent geese and a great number of little stints, among which there were a few of the much rarer Temminck's stints. There was some discussion in the hide about how to distinguish the latter from the former – the most obvious feature being the pale legs of the Temminck's and the dark ones of the little. The sharp-eyed observer may also see the shorter wing-bar of the Temminck's when it is in flight.

While we watched, there was an entertaining confrontation between a cormorant and a great black-backed gull. The cormorant had caught a flat fish (probably a flounder), but before it could secure its catch it was attacked by the gull, who grabbed the fish and tried to make off with it. The fish was so large that the gull had trouble getting airborne. Eventually he managed it and flew off, pursued by the cormorant. The pair of them flew round and round for some minutes, before the gull dropped its prize. In the end, neither of them had it – a band of gulls set upon it and tore it up between them.

From the brackish marsh we walked down towards the sea, passing through some low sand-dunes to a wide expanse of sandy beach. Here we saw some sanderlings flitting about down near the water's edge, and off shore we could see a number of eiders. One of the most fascinating features of the shore near the strand line was the remains of an ancient forest 6,000 years old, which lies almost entirely buried under the grey clay. The forest itself, or pieces of it in the form of branches and twigs, can be seen at low tide, but remnants are washed up to the strand line. If anyone insists on taking a souvenir, they are asked to take one of these pieces and not to break bits off from what is revealed at low tide.

Although it was not the right time of year, we had a look at the unique sunken hide that has been built overlooking an open area of sand and shingle. It must be very exciting during the nesting season, as it is the nesting site of a colony of little and common terns, oystercatchers and ringed plovers. During high tides in the autumn it is also the roosting ground for anything up to 30,000 waders – knots, bar-tailed godwits, oystercatchers, ringed and grey plovers, turnstones and sanderlings. The hide looks out, almost at ground level, over this area, which is roped off and looked after by a full-time warden during the nesting season.

Ranworth and Cockshoot Broads

Managing body   Norfolk Naturalists' Trust/NCC.
Access   TG 3515. 10 miles north-east of Norwich at Ranworth village, north of B1140 Acle road. Trust car-park in village opposite The Maltsters. Follow signs to centre.
Other information   Broadlands Conservation Centre open daily April – October, except Mondays. Nature trail. Leaflet.

The visitor centre at Ranworth in Norfolk must surely be the most imaginative of its kind in the country. Owned by the Norfolk Naturalists' Trust, it consists of a thatched building floating on pontoons between the Ranworth and Malthouse Broads. It is known as the Broadland Conservation Centre and contains displays, specimens and tape and slide machines explaining the natural history of the broads, and the urgent need for conservation. Upstairs is a gallery from which views of the broads and the surrounding marshland are obtained – and there are even binoculars and a telescope to help visitors watch the bird-life. Cockshoot, a short distance away, although a separate reserve is, together with Ranworth, part of the Bure Marshes National Nature Reserve, situated in the tidal reaches of the River Bure.

The Broadland Centre is approached by a 500 yard boarded nature trail showing, as the visitor walks through it, the natural succession of vegetation from open water to oak woodland. The succession starts in the water of the broad with the growth of water plants in the shallows, the roots of these stabilising and binding the mud and silt. Plants such as the pondweeds, horn-wort and waterlilies normally perform this function. But it is, sadly, a measure of the size of the problem in the broads that the quality of the water has deteriorated to such an extent that these plants have all but disappeared over recent years. They have, none the less, formed a basis for the establishment of the reed swamp, the decaying remains of which eventually form peat, and this is colonised by small bushy trees such as alder, buckthorn and guelder rose to form a swamp carr. As the distance from the water increases, the alder and sallow trees are larger, supported on thicker peat. The guide points out that there is a mixture of trees, some with single trunks, growing up to a height of about forty feet, and others with several trunks, which have been coppiced in the past.

This 'wet woodland', after a considerable number of years, finally reaches the last stage in the succession – that of oak woodland. The oak trees seen at the entrance to the nature trail are up to 250 years old, and there is an understorey of ash, holly, birch and hazel. Naturally, this dense vegetation, together with the open water of the broad, affords nest sites, food and shelter for many birds, animals and insects.

Winter is an excellent time to visit both broads, as large numbers of waterfowl arrive from September onwards, with tufted ducks, pochards, shovelers, gadwalls, mallard, goldeneyes and Bewick's swans. In very hard winters, flocks of wigeons form a day roost on the ice.

Ranworth Broad is renowned as the largest inland roost of cormorants during the winter, with up to 400 perching in the trees overlooking the water. Black-headed gulls also roost – up to 20,000 have been counted in an evening – as well as a number of great and lesser black-backed and common gulls. Winter, too, sees flocks of finches, with linnets, siskins and redpolls feeding on the seeds of alder and birches.

During spring and summer there is a great deal of activity with many nesting birds. The feral greylag and Canada geese and the mallard we saw in October nest around the water's edge, as do a few pairs of pochards and shovelers. We saw a great crested grebe – another nesting species that moves in early to establish its territory; and Slavonian, red and black-necked grebes have also been recorded. April sees the return of some of the common terns from Africa, to nest on three fibreglass islands which have been placed there for them. Up to thirty-five pairs have availed themselves of this facility. Black terns are sometimes seen in June and September.

From the gallery of the Broadland Centre, we saw a number of herons on the far side of the water, and there is a small heronry in the alders with up to fifteen nests. From here we also saw the nearly-submerged hulks of two Norfolk wherries (wooden sailing boats) and coal barges that have been sunk near the bank in an attempt to stop erosion by wave action set up by the hundreds of pleasure boats.

Coots and moorhens were present in appreciable numbers during our visit, but, although water rails breed at the reserve, we neither saw nor heard any. While a bittern is occasionally seen, it is a tragic fact that the only sight most people will have of one of these fascinating birds is the museum specimen in the centre. There are, I understand, less than six breeding pairs left in Norfolk – a statistic attributable

One of the great problems of the Broads is the bank erosion by the wash of pleasure boats.

almost wholly to the pollution and disturbance of the broads.

There are small birds in abundance, the thick vegetation providing excellent cover for them. In the oak woodland, willow warblers, chiffchaffs and blackcaps are seen, and we saw a number of tits, tree-creepers, a great spotted woodpecker and a nuthatch. The reed-beds contain numbers of nesting reed buntings, and reed and sedge warblers; the reed warblers often acting as hosts for cuckoos.

The birds of prey most likely to be seen are kestrels (we watched one for some time on our way along the river bank to Cockshoot Broad), sparrow-hawks, an occasional marsh harrier and, in the winter, hen harriers. Ospreys have been recorded on passage.

From Ranworth Broad we travelled the short distance to the riverside car-park at Woodbastwick, and walked along the bank towards Cockshoot Broad. We were struck by the amount of traffic on the river, and as the pleasure boats went past, we could see just how much disturbance the waves they created caused. No wonder erosion on the broads is a problem, with hundreds and hundreds of them passing to and fro, and not just during the summer months.

We turned off the main riverbank and crossed a foot-bridge on to the walkway that led beside Cockshoot Dyke to a hide overlooking Cockshoot Broad itself. It is a lovely place – quiet, secluded and surrounded by beautiful woodland.

The two reserves are certainly rewarding in terms of birds at most times of the year, and they are also important for plants and insects. In such a damp habitat, mosses, lichens and ferns grow in profusion. Most of the typical marsh and wetland plants are found, but there are several of more than usual interest. The marsh pea –

rare throughout Britain – occurs, while cowbane, marsh sowthistle and bog myrtle are also seen.

One of the most significant of the plants is milk parsley, the food plant of the swallowtail butterfly – which is the largest British butterfly and confined to the Norfolk Broads. It breeds on the reserve. Other butterflies include the holly blue, painted lady and common, while moths are represented by the vapourer, puss moth and elephant hawk.

Dragonflies have declined in numbers over the years, and a national rarity, the Norfolk dragonfly, *Aeshna isoceles*, is found in only a few places on the broads. Rather too apparent, and less attractive in every way, are the numbers of mosquitoes and the biting cleg fly *Haematopota pluvialis*.

An attractive mammal of the broads is the Chinese water deer, which lives chiefly in the alder carr, where it browses on shoots and young trees.

Cley Marshes

Managing body   Norfolk Naturalists' Trust.
Access   TG 0545. Adjoins A149 Wells – Cromer road east of Cley village.
Other information   Car-park. Permit from visitor centre. Hides. Leaflet.

The North Norfolk coast is an irresistible place for naturalists in general and birdwatchers in particular. It is only a slight exaggeration to say that it is possible to go along this lovely coast from Holme-next-the-Sea in the west to Sheringham – a distance of 30 miles – and remain on nature reserve land throughout.

Having visited Snettisham and Titchwell on the Wash, we travelled along the coast to the Norfolk Naturalists' reserve at Cley Marshes. We parked by the visitor centre, which looks out over the reserve to the shingle bank bordering the sea. There are various routes leading through grazing marsh and extensive reed-beds to the nine hides, including one for the public and another for disabled visitors.

Crossing the road from the centre, we went through the wet pasture and the reed-beds, pausing to look at the flock of feral greylag geese that were on the move between grazing grounds. From the three hides overlooking Whitwell and Simmonds Scrapes, and Pets and South Pools we saw a variety of wildfowl, with hundreds of wigeons and smaller numbers of teal, pintails, shovelers, redshanks and dunlins.

Returning to the road, we went the short distance from the

visitor centre to the public hide. We soon spotted a snipe on a small grassy promontory close to the hide. As we watched, another appeared from behind a clump of grass, then another – and in the end we counted a dozen in this small area. Moving on to the far side of the reserve, we walked along the top of the East Bank boundary to Bittern Hide, where we hoped to see one of these elusive birds. We were out of luck, however, and went on along the bank to a point overlooking Arnold's Marsh to the right. This proved to be a good area for waders, with redshanks, dunlins, ringed plovers, a grey plover and turnstones. Other species recorded include the common sandpiper, and in autumn and spring rarities are often seen.

Reaching the next hides – North and Maynard – involved a third of a mile trek along the shingle behind the high bank separating the main part of the reserve from the sea. On our left was some low-lying marshy land which seemed ideal for waders, but was deserted. From the hides we looked out over the water-filled North Scrape, which was alive with wigeons, pintails, shelducks and shovelers. A walk down the western border of the reserve to the beach was rewarding, with sightings of a very late common tern, a glaucous gull and several red-throated divers.

We only saw a small proportion of the many species recorded at Cley throughout the year. These are described in the reserve leaflet, and, for the benefit of others who visit this exciting reserve, a brief résumé of what can be seen might be useful.

At the beginning of the year, winter wildfowl, in addition to those we saw during our visit, may include red-breasted mergansers, long-tailed ducks and goldeneyes on the deeper pools, together with some brent geese if food elsewhere is in short supply. Whooper swans are rarer visitors.

Spring is an exciting time, with migrants such as ruffs, black-tailed godwits, chiffchaffs, wheatears, and sedge and reed warblers. Sandwich terns may be seen on Arnold's Marsh at this time and in the autumn. Migratory species continue to arrive or pass through during May and June – May is of special interest, with waders such as Kentish plovers and Temminck's stints en route for the Arctic, black terns, and the more unusual woodchat, bee-eater and tawny pipit. Spoonbills sometimes appear in June, while breeding birds include ringed plovers, oystercatchers, garganeys, shelducks and gadwalls, together with avocets, bitterns and bearded tits.

From mid-July, greenshanks, whimbrels, little ringed plovers and golden plovers arrive, with large numbers of sandpipers – green, wood and common. Little stints and curlew sandpipers often come in appreciable numbers, while pectoral sandpipers are seen most years.

We were rewarded with the sight of a red-throated diver off the beach at Cley.

The North Norfolk coast is outstanding for rarities – many of which are seen at Cley – icterine and aquatic warblers have been recorded, and birds such as the Asian slender-billed nutcracker and a Pallas's warbler have been seen.

It is a good place, too, for sea-birds, with the autumn storms ensuring an impressive list – gannets, shearwaters, petrels, kittiwakes and skuas. In October, snow buntings are often a feature along the shingle ridge, while the westward movement of rooks, jackdaws, chaffinches and lapwings produces remarkable numbers. At night, it is said, the sky is sometimes full of redwings, blackbirds, goldcrests and fieldfares.

In winter the wildfowl arrive, and large numbers of Bewick's swans are seen passing along the coast on their way from Siberia to the Ouse Washes and Welney. There is no doubt at all that Cley is one of the best birdwatching sites in the country at virtually any time of the year.

Cley Marshes is also of interest to botanists, as it shows a clear zonation of plants according to the varying salinity of the soil, as it increases in concentration from the coast road behind the reserve to a maximum at the shingle ridge at the seaward boundary. In the north of the reserve, where some of the land is still subject to flooding by the sea, the extremely salt conditions support sea lavender, sea aster, rice grass, and sea arrowgrass. On the shingle bank, sea thrift and campion, yellow horned poppy and curled dock are seen, while shrubby seablite and grey hairgrass are found almost at their northern limits.

In the saltpans and along some of the old drainage channels where the salinity increases in summer due to evaporation, such plants as sea sandwort and sea poa grow; while in the less saline areas of the marsh, the more brackish conditions support sea plantain, mud rush and the water crowfoot, *Ranunculus baudotii*. The reed-beds are of the common reed found in the fresh and brackish water, while in the more or less fresh water of the dykes and the edges of the marsh grass where fresh water comes from springs, false fox-sedge, sea-club rush, great reed mace and bur-reed grow.

From Cley, it is possible to walk the three miles or so along the shingle beach to Blakeney Point, another magnificent place for birds, and a National Nature Reserve. We took a boat trip from Blakeney to see the seals on the sand-bar off the Point. As we approached, huge flocks of birds got off – dunlins, knots, oystercatchers and many others that were too far away to identify with any certainty.

We landed briefly on the reserve and from there looked across to the Point, which was covered with birds, while brent geese were in the lagoon. On the journey back after a close look at a dozen or so common seals, we saw a great northern diver in the harbour.

Hickling Broad
National Nature Reserve

Managing body   Norfolk Naturalists' Trust/NCC.
Access   TG 4121. From Greyhound Inn at Hickling Green follow road signed 'No access to Broad', then take third turning right at cross-roads.
Other information   Open daily (except Tuesday) 1 April – 31 October. Permit from warden at site entrance. Nature trails. Water trails (mid-week June – September). Leaflets and guides.

We visited this reserve (most of which is managed by the Norfolk Naturalists' Trust) out of season, but as we were in the area, it seemed a pity to miss it altogether. As it turned out, we were unlucky; due to exceptionally high winds and rough weather, most of the birds that had been there had temporarily departed for more sheltered surroundings. Nevertheless, we were not wholly unrewarded.

There are two land-based nature trails, pamphlets for which can be obtained from the warden's office at the entrance to the reserve, and there is also a water trail by boat – not available while we were there. We decided to follow the Deary's nature trail of a mile and a quarter described in the pamphlet.

We drove from the warden's house along the road across the marshes leading to the car-park, keeping a look-out in case of marsh harriers hunting, but we did not see any at this time. From the car-park, armed with the key to the various hides, we crossed the bridge over a dyke to a path, which was lined with small trees and bushes where reed and sedge warblers, willow warblers and redpolls may be seen. Our first stop was at the Warden's Observation Hut – a high hide with good all-round viewing across the colossal reed-beds. There were a few coots on the waterways between the reeds, and at appropriate times common and little terns and cormorants may be seen fishing.

In front of the hut were two wader pools, where in late summer greenshanks, spotted redshanks, wood and green sandpipers and dunlins may be seen. Of the ducks, mallard and a couple of gadwalls were present; while others to be seen at various times include teal, shovelers, shelducks and the occasional garganey. We had a brief sight of a kingfisher as it settled momentarily on one of the posts provided before flashing off into the reeds again. Marsh harriers, bearded tits and bitterns may also be seen from this hide.

Exceptionally high winds had driven most of the birds from Hickling; on a better day we might have seen a greenshank.

We left the main track to take the short circular reed-bed walk to the third post on the trail. Bordering the walk are various plants such as giant water dock, meadow-sweet and flag iris. Here, it is possible to see or hear reed and sedge warblers, bearded tits and, very occasionally, a Savi's warbler. This is one of the places on the reserve frequented by the swallowtail butterfly.

Returning to the main pathway, our next stop was at Deary's West Hide, which is sited above the north floodbank of the Broad and overlooks a wader pool, the water of which is controlled by sluices. This is a good nesting area for such species as the lapwing, redshank, ringed plover and the terns; it has, from time to time, attracted a visiting spoonbill. We were quietly amused at the request in the pamphlet not to lock other visitors in the hide – we had visions of rather cross birdwatchers being marooned in this very isolated place for some time!

Retracing our steps, we crossed the bridge over the dyke and followed the path, along which grasshopper warblers are sometimes heard, and Oak eggar moths seen, before turning left down a short track to Deary's East Hide on the opposite side of the wader pool. Temminck's stints are regularly seen in spring and autumn – and we thought we saw a wood sandpiper in front of a hide diagonally opposite.

We returned to the main path and turned off right to Cadbury's Hide, which overlooks a new pool constructed in 1982 to encourage little terns to nest there instead of their traditional nesting site in the Broad which is subject to flooding. Only two pairs have done so, but there was the unexpected bonus of a pair of avocets.

Champion's East Hide overlooks another wader pool in which the level of the water is controlled to give shallower water in spring and autumn for the waders, and deeper for the ducks, such as gadwalls, teal, shelducks, mallard, shovelers and sometimes Bewick's swans. Of the passerines, migrating yellow wagtails, whinchats and wheatears may be seen here, as well as on other parts of the reserve.

Finally, we walked back to the main road to the car-park with the marshes on our right where, in spring, nesting snipe, lapwings, skylarks and redshanks are seen and, at migration times, various passerines and also ruffs. We went back to the Warden's Observation Hut for a final look – and how fortunate that we did. As we rounded a bend, a male marsh harrier got up suddenly quite close to us and we had a good, if rather brief, view of it before it disappeared behind some trees. This was not the only one we were to see; as we drove back along the road towards the exit we saw another male hunting low and slowly over the marshes to our right.

This one we managed to keep in sight for quite some time as it hawked purposefully up and down before flapping off towards the centre of the reserve.

These impressive birds are a marvellous sight. They are one of the rarest of British breeding species, with under thirty pairs, are restricted to East Anglia and are the largest of the harriers. The darker females are easily distinguished by the striking pale head and throat, while the male has large blue-grey wing patches and tail. The hunting flight is characteristically low and slow, with the wings held in an unmistakable V-shape when gliding in between the slow wing flaps.

The courtship of the marsh harrier is spectacular, with the male soaring up to 700 feet or more, then diving and somersaulting down. The nest, built on the ground usually among the reed-beds, is made of twigs and aquatic vegetation, and the four or five pale blue eggs are incubated by the female. She may fly up to meet the male during incubation, taking food from him in a thrilling aerial pass.

We hope to return to Hickling, not just to see the birds that had so inconveniently departed this time, but to take the water trail – surely the best possible way of seeing a reserve in broadland.

Welney Wildfowl Refuge

Managing body   Wildfowl Trust.
Access   TL 5595. South side of Ouse Washes, 1¾ miles north-east of bridge on A1101 Welney – Littleport road.
Other information   Visitors report to centre on arrival. Entrance fee for non-members. Open daily except 24 and 25 December. Escorted tours on Saturday and Sunday by arrangement. Literature.

For anyone who wants to have a really close look at genuinely wild wildfowl at close quarters and from the comfort of a heated observatory, then the Wildfowl Trust's Welney Refuge is the place for them. There are also about fifty other small hides from which the birds may be observed.

Welney consists of approximately 800 acres of water-meadows within the Ouse Washes in Norfolk, and in winter there may be up to 2,000 Bewick's swans and 200 whoopers – many of them visible from the observatory and hides. None of the Welney birds are captive – although they are fed daily with just enough potatoes and grain to encourage them to stay around the lagoon, so that they may be seen, identified and studied. The remainder of their food comes from foraging over the nearby farmland.

From the visitor centre on one side of the road, where there is an interesting display, the visitor takes a key to the covered footbridge on the opposite side. This leads across the Hundred Foot Drain or New Bedford River to the observatory complex. Access to the paths to the other hides is also gained from here.

In front of the observatory is the main lagoon, the excavation of which was one of the first things to be done when the refuge was established. It is large enough to allow the landing and taking off of the swans, and the depth of the water is controlled by gates. When we were there, it was a mass of swans and ducks. There were dozens of Bewick's, a few whoopers, some mutes, and a large variety of ducks – wigeons, mallard, teal, one or two pintails, shovelers, pochards and some coots. According to the booklet available at the visitor centre, a typical winter daily count could be as many as 10,000 wigeons, 3,000 mallard, 1,500 teal, 500 pochards and 200 pintails. The wigeons come from Russia, the majority of the teal and shovelers from the Baltic and the pochards from eastern Europe.

Although all the wildfowl are truly wild, they are well aware of the times when the food arrives, congregating in great masses below the windows of the observatory, waiting for the warden with his wheelbarrow to arrive. It is a scrabbling, competitive mass of

Shelducks are just one of over sixty nesting species at Welney Wildfowl Refuge.

birds, all trying to get their share.

The principal aim of the refuge has been to attract and increase the numbers of Bewick's swans, using management techniques pioneered at Slimbridge. The swans were at risk as a species because of the loss of their traditional feeding grounds. It is known that the Bewick's breed around the Kara Sea in northern Russia, and that their migratory flights to Britain, over 2,300 miles, are undertaken at speeds of up to 50 miles per hour and at heights of up to 5,000 feet. Breeding starts when they are four to six years old and it has been shown by work at Slimbridge and Welney that the most successful breeders are those in the best condition. It has also been shown that when the swans return to Welney or Slimbridge or any other centre, the cygnets arrive with their parents and stay with them during the winter – thus helping the youngsters to become familiar with the migration routes. In the wild, Bewick's may live for over twenty years. Each bird can be recognised by means of the yellow markings on the bill, and the fact that some easily identifiable birds return year after year has provided valuable information about their habits.

Other birds that visit Welney during the winter include cormorants, of which we saw a number. Geese, usually white-fronted, sometimes stay for a short period, while short-eared owls and hen harriers are regularly seen. Marsh harriers are seen in the summer and autumn. Other less common raptors include the merlin, sparrow-hawk and peregrine.

The central observatory at Welney has two unheated wings, like huge hides, with viewing flaps giving extensive views over the reserve. These may, for some people, perhaps provide a welcome relief from the crowd in the heated room. We spent some time in both, before going out onto the screened walks which lead to the smaller hides in the banks and in the 'fingers' of the banks on either side of the observatory. From these, we were able to see the south and the north lagoons, the World Wildlife Scrape and the wader ponds.

Welney is open throughout the year, and although the winter is obviously the most spectacular time, it is certainly not without attractions in the summer. Summer migrants use it as a stop-over on their way north; these include such species as stints, sandpipers, greenshanks and bar-tailed godwits.

When the breeding season begins, with over sixty nesting species, the refuge is certainly not dull. Lapwings are present, together with redshanks, ruffs, reed and sedge warblers, reed buntings, the occasional black tern, and the ducks – mallard, shovelers, garganeys, pintails, wigeons, tufteds, gadwalls and shelducks. Perhaps the most exciting are the black-tailed godwits and the ruffs, which have returned to this part of the Washes as well as to the RSPB section. The number of pairs of godwits nesting at Welney rose to twenty in 1982.

During the summer, provided conditions are suitable, visitors may go on an extended walk across the Washes to the River Delph on the opposite side of the refuge. This provides an opportunity to see more of the habitats at close quarters, and enjoy some of the rich botanical life to be found. Over 260 species of flowering plants have been recorded, and of special interest are some of the aquatics. There are, for instance, in the ditches, no less than 16 species and hybrids of pondweed, and other plants include arrowhead, water crowfoot, water parsnip, duckweed, frogbit and fringed water lily. Along the screened bank and the summer walk, a number of the plants are labelled. Butterflies also occur in profusion in spring and summer.

Welney is a fascinating place, and the more people able to visit it and support the work that is going on there, and at the other Wildfowl Trust establishments, the better.

The Ouse Washes RSPB Reserve

Managing body   RSPB/Cambridge & Isle of Ely Naturalist's Trust.
Access   TL 4886. Signposted from Manea. Take the B1093 from Wimblington or B1098 from Chatteris (both off A141 Chatteris/March road).
Other information   Car-park at Welches Dam RSPB visitor centre. Leaflet. Access at all times. Best viewing in afternoon.

The RSPB reserve at the Ouse Washes is a thrilling place for the birdwatcher. Not only are there spectacular numbers of birds and a wide variety of species, but the layout of the reserve and the eleven hides ensures an unusual measure of sustained excitement. The bulk of the reserve – the Washes themselves – lies hidden from view behind a high bank. Although it is often possible to hear the sound of hundreds of birds while walking behind the bank, they can only be seen from the hides. These are set into the bank at intervals and carefully situated so that the view from each shows a different aspect of the reserve.

Before setting off for the first hide, we spent quite a time in the visitor centre, studying the displays which explain a great deal about how the reserve is managed. We could not have chosen a better time, for the young volunteer warden had just spotted a short-eared owl in a tree behind the centre, and we had a marvellous view of it.

From the centre we crossed the bridge over the Old Bedford river and turned left to walk along behind the high bank to the first hide. Immediately on the other side of the bank, as we saw from the hide, is another river – the Delph – running parallel to the Old Bedford. There is yet a third river, which runs parallel to the other two but on the far side of the Washes. The Old and New Bedford are, in fact, two huge drains, built in the seventeenth century for the Earl of Bedford by the Dutch engineer, Cornelius Vermuyden, in an attempt to drain the fens. His aim was to straighten the tortuous path of the Great Ouse river and so divert the winter floodwaters into the low-lying meadowland between the two new rivers instead of into the rich soils of the surrounding fenland. The meadowland is traversed by a series of small drainage ditches running at right angles between the rivers.

The meadows are on a slight upward gradient from the Old to the New Bedford river, and in the winter, when the tidal water of the New Bedford is high, sluices are opened and the water flows into the ditches and discharges into the Delph. Flooding often occurs, not just in winter, but in summer as well. In the summer, if there is no flooding, the ditches act as 'wet fences' between each individual 'wash' and the meadows are used for grazing animals.

Our first excitement was the distant sound of wigeons, which came nearer and nearer, and as we looked up, we saw small flocks of them overhead, following the line of the river. Then more and more came, until the sky overhead seemed to be full of them. It was a spectacular sight and a wonderful sound. The Washes are the wintering grounds for enormous numbers of these attractive wildfowl – an incredible 42,500 have been recorded, and the average is nearly 36,000 (about a quarter of the British population). We hurried on to the hide and, just a short distance from it, we heard another marvellous sound – the haunting call of whooper swans. We rushed into the hide and raised the flaps as quickly as we dared, just in time to see half a dozen of these superb birds flying past, low over the Washes. There is something very special about the sound of whoopers – a sound that seems to match the beautiful desolation of the Washes.

One of the principal advantages of the Washes is that their gradient ensures varying depths of water, which, except at maximum flooding, allows a range of wetland habitats – from meadowland, to water shelving from a few inches to several feet in depth. On the far side of the meadows we could distinguish hundreds of wigeons, grazing among the tussocky grassland. We also picked out a single greylag goose, and a number of mute swans on land, on the water of the ditches and in the flooded areas. Several tufted ducks and some coots were swimming up and down the river in front of us, and one or two moorhens were at the water's edge. A few mallard and some teal were on the flooded area.

We moved on to the next hide, where we saw much more. At the edge of the water there were a dozen or more snipe probing away, together with some redshanks, a few more of which flighted in while we were watching. After a few minutes about half a dozen ruffs flew in and began feeding at the edge. Ruffs are one of several species which have re-established themselves as breeding species on the Ouse. They returned in the 1960s and a few pairs breed each year; their extraordinary display may be seen each spring.

From this hide a great number of wildfowl could be seen, part of the nationally important number which come every winter. In addition to the wigeons already mentioned, maximum numbers are impressive: 3,650 pintails, 1,070 shovelers, 5,500 pochards, 7,000 mallard and 7,570 teal have been recorded. Naturally, we saw only some, but they were a magnificent sight. My favourites are the elegant pintails, with their lovely, delicate colouring.

As we moved up the line of hides, we had different views of the Washes, and, from time to time, flights of whoopers came over, and a few Bewick's. Our one disappointment was that the main body of Bewick's – of which there can be over 3,000 – were not there. Most of them were, it seems, along at Welney. One hide we all but shared with a male kestrel which came stooping down, presumably misjudged its direction and very nearly flew straight in the open viewing flaps!

While winter sees the greatest numbers of birds, the Ouse Washes are by no means deserted in the spring and summer. There are some very interesting breeding birds, with a total of over sixty species; the ruffs have already been mentioned, and of at least equal interest are the black-tailed godwits. These were found to be nesting on the reserve in 1952, having only been known to nest in Britain about half a dozen times in the preceding hundred years. The numbers have gradually increased, and the Washes are now Britain's principal breeding site for them, with an annual figure of forty to sixty pairs. Their spectacular courtship, including the unusual 'butterfly' display, begins as soon as they arrive. Black terns have also bred from time to time. Of the other waders, large numbers of snipe breed, as do lapwings and redshanks; and the wildfowl include mallard, small numbers of tufted ducks, pochards, gadwalls and teal, and a few pairs of garganeys. The Washes are also one of the few British breeding sites for pintails.

Although the washes are associated with wildfowl and waders, there are, of course, many smaller birds. In fact the reserve is one of the biggest breeding sites in the country for yellow wagtails, with

Ruffs are one of several species which have re-established
themselves as breeding species on the Washes. Their extraordinary
display is seen in spring.

over 200 pairs. There are also about 400 pairs of meadow pipits, and
smaller numbers of redpolls, goldfinches, reed and sedge warblers
and reed buntings. Stock doves and little owls nest in holes in the
crack willows, and there is a heronry.

Management of such a reserve is of prime importance, and the
display in the visitor centre gives much interesting information
about this, as does the RSPB leaflet. Visitors at certain times of the
year will quickly become aware of at least one feature of
management – the grazing of sheep, which are frequently met
when walking to the hides. A regular programme of grazing by
these, together with horses and cattle, is practised. They help to
control the length of the sward, which is an important feature of
wildfowl food. Hay is cut before the animals are turned out onto
the fields.

The provision of suitable and attractive areas of water of different types is vital to the breeding success of ducks and waders, and for the requirements of the wintering birds. The various types of pools have either been excavated mechanically, been created by using herbicides on dense monocultures to form shallow, mudbased lagoons, or by flooding the lower-lying land. Water plant communities in the ditches are maintained and diversified by a regime of rotational clearing; and the digging of new ditches parallel to the existing ones provides more nesting sites for ducks. The osier beds are also managed on a rotational basis, being cut to provide a variety of age ranges and thus a range of nesting sites. The young crack willows are pollarded to prolong their lives and, incidentally, to provide nesting sites for barn owls and mallard.

Wales

South Stack RSPB Reserve

Managing body   RSPB.
Access   SH 2182. Road to cliffs signposted from Holyhead.
Other information   Car-parks. Information centre open daily April – August.
Leaflets at centre or from RSPB.

A perfect summer day is rare in Britain, but we were lucky enough
to spend two on the RSPB reserve at South Stack Cliffs on Anglesey.
Conditions were idyllic, with clear almost cloudless skies; a sea of
deep, yet bright, blue made the dramatic white sandstone of
Holyhead Mountain dazzling in its brilliance; and the heather was a
glowing purple carpet.

The coastal scenery at South Stack, on the north-west tip of
Anglesey Island, is magnificent. Sheer cliffs rise almost 400 feet
out of the sea, which, over the centuries, has gouged out deep
chasms and caves in the cliff-faces, and isolated tower-like off-shore
stacks. Massive earth movements have made giant folds in the
Cambrian rocks of the cliff-faces, dramatic examples of which can
be seen from the small island on which the South Stack lighthouse
stands.

The geological formation of the cliffs, especially the two large
buttresses between the lighthouse and the RSPB centre at Ellin's
Tower, is such that flat ledges, formed by differential weathering of
two types of rock, offer ideal sites for nesting sea-birds, particularly
auks. These same cliffs are also a great challenge to the climbing
fraternity, although the RSPB has been able to negotiate a voluntary
ban on rock-climbing, helicopter exercises and canoeing, with the
relevant authorities for the duration of the breeding season each
year.

The South Stack Reserve is split into two separate parts – the
spectacular Holyhead Mountain area overlooking the cliff-fringed
Gogarth Bay and guarded at either end by the North and South
Stacks and, a mile or so to the south, the lower-lying headland of
Penrhos Feilw Common. The latter is less spectacular, but of great
beauty, and a delightful place, especially for the botanist.

From the car-park at the reserve, well-made tracks lead through the heather to the RSPB centre where visitors may obtain leaflets describing the birds, plants, insects and geology of the area. The centre, with its wonderful views of the coastline, is only a few yards from the cliff edge – an edge that is guarded along a considerable part of its length by a comforting low bank (provided by the RSPB), from which masses of the sea-birds can be seen. At the time of our visit, the rocky ledges of the two principal buttresses near the lighthouse were packed with guillimots, of which some 2,000 pairs nest annually. Razorbills were less obvious because of their preference for the crevices rather than the ledges themselves, but approximately 600 pairs nest. Of the 200 or so pairs of puffins, a few had ventured onto the ledges from the nesting burrows, and, as we watched, there was a constant passage of all three auks flying busily to and from the cliffs, their raucous cries clearly audible.

A short walk around the cliff edge brought us to a flight of steps down to the lighthouse. Daunting though the prospect of the climb back up may be, it is well worth it. On the way down we had closer views of the auks, not just on the ledges, but on the sea at the foot of the cliffs and around the lighthouse island. An added bonus was the wild flowers, growing over every part of the cliff where there was any soil, giving the appearance of a natural rock-garden – a delightful and colourful sight.

At the bottom of the steps, a bridge leads across to the lighthouse island, from where we had an impressive view of the almost grotesque folds in the Cambrian rocks of the cliffs; the power of the movement that caused them is quite beyond imagination. Back on the cliff-top once more, we were fortunate enough to see a small party of the other birds for which the reserve is renowned – choughs. They came flashing up from below the cliff edge uttering their strange calls, and landed on the grass near a party of picnickers.

On the bright sunny day they looked so handsome with their gleaming, iridescent blue-black plumage, striking crimson legs and down-curved bills. Apparently unperturbed by the presence of people, they probed about in the heather, grass and gorse, looking for insects, and as the sunlight caught their plumage at different angles, the greenish tinge of their tails and wings became apparent. Quite soon, the little party took off again, and, following them to the cliff edge, we enjoyed watching their wonderfully agile display of flying, their spectacular manoeuvrability aided by their very deeply slotted wing-tips. Some of their antics were reminiscent of ravens as they dived and soared, flipping over and dropping down steeply before levelling out and flashing up again, then repeating the performance – apparently for the sheer joy of it!

1 **Above** The lagoon at Farlington is a haven for a significant number of wildfowl and other birds, while in the reed-beds sedge and reed warblers nest.

2 **Right** The great spotted wood-pecker is much more often seen than its smaller relative, the lesser-spotted. The drumming of the latter is much faster (14-15 blows per second) compared with 8-10 of the larger bird.

3 **Above** One of the quiet backwaters at Radipole, situated in the middle of Weymouth in Dorset.

4 **Opposite (top)** Thinning of woodland at reserves such as Fore Wood allows the establishment of an understorey which offers nesting sites for small birds like the blackcap.

5 **Opposite (centre)** One of the most marvellous sights of bird-watching along coasts and estuaries is the great flocks of dunlins wheeling and turning in perfect unison, flashing first white then grey.

6 **Opposite (bottom)** Dungeness is a splendid place for seeing large numbers of migrants such as chiffchaffs in an area that is overgrown with sallow.

7 **Above** Among the fixed dunes at Braunton Burrows are areas of the lovely pale yellow evening primrose.

8 **Left** The nest of the reed warbler is woven around the stems of reeds. It is very deep and has no support from below.

9 **Opposite (top)** We were very lucky to see a pair of great crested grebes in full breeding plumage at Radipole Lake where they nest.

10 **Opposite (bottom)** Sparrowhawks are quite often seen at Arne in Dorset, and breed, among other places, at Gelli Hir in Wales — the nest usually consisting of birch or larch twigs.

11 **Opposite (top)** Welney offers a close look at wildfowl. Like the smaller Bewick's swans, these whoopers may be identified by their individual beak markings.

12 **Opposite (bottom)** In spite of the redshanks' maddening habit of alerting everything else in the area to even the stealthiest bird-watcher, how we would miss them if they disappeared from our coasts.

13 **Left** Common though they are, it is always a pleasure to see herons. We much enjoyed watching one cope with a very large eel at Titchwell. Stithians is also a good place to see these statuesque birds.

14 **Below** A view of the Ouse Washes from one of the hides, looking towards the New Bedford river.

15 **Above** We always associate siskins with Minsmere, as our visit there was one of the few occasions when we actually saw birds after being told by others of their presence.

16 **Left** At Titchwell Marsh we enjoyed watching a battle between a cormorant and a greater black-backed gull over a flat fish. At Penderi we were able to study the differences between cormorants and shags.

17 **Right** The interior of a long-tailed tit's nest is lined with feathers, and the incredible total of 2,000 feather-collecting journeys has been recorded in the construction of a nest.

18 **Below** As we climbed through the Gwenffrwd reserve we paused to look back across the valley and enjoyed the varying greens of the hills as the sunlight and cloud made dappled patterns on them.

19 **Above** We saw tree-creepers in many woodland reserves. These delightful little birds have been likened to mice as they scurry up and round tree trunks.

20 **Opposite (top left)** Dinas is in red kite country, and although we did not see one there, we enjoyed the boulder-strewn stream and the magnificent scenery.

21 **Opposite (top right)** Not surprisingly, we saw jackdaws almost everywhere we went. Out of the breeding season we sometimes saw them flocking with rooks.

22 **Opposite (bottom)** By dint of crawling up the shingle bank from the bay side and peering cautiously over, we could see the masses of terns which breed on the island in the pool at Cemlyn.

23 **Above (left)** The little stretch of stream between the bank and the nearest island at Beltingham makes a charming picture of a peaceful backwater.

24 **Above (right)** Snipe are common, but it is always a pleasure to see them and to listen to the weird sound of their 'drumming' – the sound made by the vibration of the outer tail feathers.

25 **Left** Turnstones use their feet to hold down molluscs while they extract the contents of the shell with their strong bills.

26 There are four sturdily built and strongly railed observation platforms at St Bees so that visitors can look right over the cliff edge at the sea-birds roosting on the ledges below.

27 The plaintive 'peep' of oystercatchers always evokes thought of estuaries such as the Exe, and of great wader places such as Snettisham and Morecambe.

28 **Left** The story of the return of the osprey to Loch Garten is an epic chapter in British ornithology.

29 **Below** Loch Muick on the Glen Muick and Lochnagar reserve is set in country of breath-taking beauty. We took the eight-mile walk around the loch and it was worth every step!

30 **Opposite (top)** Fowlsheugh has been described as a 'sea-bird city'. The cliff-faces are absolutely crammed with birds during the breeding season. Seen here are razorbills, guillimots and kittiwakes.

31 **Opposite (bottom)** One of the delightful views we enjoyed during our guided walk in the woods surrounding Lochs Garten and Mallachie.

32 The ptarmigan is a typical bird of the Scottish Highlands – seen here in summer plumage, it is completely white in winter.

33 It was sheer joy to watch and listen to the barnacle geese at Caerlaverock as they grazed and then took to the air, moving to a new grazing ground.

Two hundred or so pairs of puffins nest at South Stack, as well as 2,000 pairs of guillimots and about 600 pairs of razorbills.

The choughs breed at South Stack, the nest of heather, twigs and seaweed being concealed in the dark caves of the cliffs. The female lays an average of four eggs, which hatch some seventeen or eighteen days later. The youngsters are fed by regurgitation, and remain in the nest for up to five weeks. When fledged, they have dark brownish plumage and orange bills.

Our party of choughs headed off towards North Stack at the other end of the reserve, and, although we saw them again from time to time, we saw no sign of the few ravens that are present along this stretch of cliff.

The area between North and South Stack is mostly heathland, with many rocky outcrops, and we could never remember having seen heather of such a vivid purple colour. We searched (I suspect in the wrong places) for one of the botanical rarities of the reserve, the spotted rock rose, but were too late in the year to see another scarce plant, the maritime sub-species of the field fleawort. The birds were interesting rather than dramatic, and we saw considerable numbers of stonechats, whinchats, meadow pipits, and wrens, and, near the cliff edge, some rock pipits.

Returning from North Stack, we made our way from Ellin's Tower along the cliff-top and watched the kittiwakes and an occasional fulmar flying in and out of their nesting sites on Penlas Rock just off shore. Inconveniently for the birdwatcher they have chosen to nest on the seaward side, but as the colony is reportedly increasing year by year, perhaps in due course they will expand their territories to the shore side.

A short drive took us to Penrhos Feilw Common, and although we saw relatively little in the way of bird-life except a few oystercatchers and lapwings, with gulls off shore, waders such as whimbrels, dotterels and greenshanks are seen on passage at migration times, while merlins and short-eared owls, also on passage, use the area as a hunting ground.

The Common is well known for its flora, and it is a rare example in Wales of maritime vegetation such as is found much further south in North Cornwall and the Isles of Scilly. Exposure to the very fierce salt-laden winds has resulted in the heather, bell heather and dwarf gorse growing in an interesting wave-like formation.

At the height of the breeding season, which coincides with the beginning of the holiday season, South Stack is hardly the place for the birdwatcher who enjoys isolation. However, the RSPB has capitalised on its easy accessibility to crowds of people who would probably not count themselves as regular birdwatchers. The reserve has certainly been developed to allow people to see some of the most attractive sea-birds easily and safely.

Cemlyn Bay Reserve

Managing body   North Wales Naturalists' Trust.
Access   SH 3393. Turn off A5025 at Tregele for Cemlyn. Two car-parks – at Treath Cemlyn on east side and Bryn Aberon on west.
Other information   Special request not to walk along top of shingle bank during nesting season.

This is a delightful reserve – compact, interesting and with a remarkable range of wildlife within its thirty-five acres. It consists of a shingle bank or 'bay bar' formed from storm beach shingle, behind which is a brackish pool containing several small, low islands. There is a good range of bird-life throughout the year.

We visited in the spring, and by crawling up the shingle bank from the bay side and peering cautiously over, we could see the hundreds of terns which breed on the islands in the pool. The majority were Arctic and common, but there were also a few Sandwich – and up to 750 pairs may nest in a good season. The ubiquitous black-headed gulls also breed there. In and round the pool we saw shelducks, oystercatchers, redshanks and mallard. At the far end of the bay, several red-breasted mergansers (another breeding species) were bobbing about on the sea, and half a dozen

Peering cautiously over the shingle bank at Cemlyn Bay, we could
see the masses of nesting terns, including Arctic.

ringed plovers were scuttling around on the sand and seaweed
near the rocky outcrops. We were lucky to be there on a really
glorious day, and it was a joy to sit on the shingle, watching the
mergansers and ringed plovers, and keeping a look-out for other
passing sea-birds.

In the winter, the bay and the pool offer refuge and food for a
selection of birds – mallard, shovelers, teal, wigeons and the diving
ducks such as goldeneyes. Little grebes and mergansers are also
seen, while waders such as dunlins, turnstones and both grey and
golden plovers are recorded. Bewick's and whooper swans
occasionally visit in the winter.

The merganser is one of our favourite birds, not only are they
handsome, but they so often pop up when we least expect them –
from Scotland to Cornwall – and have frequently provided
welcome relief in an otherwise barren day. The serrated hooked
bill of the merganser enables the bird to grasp fish, the main item of
diet, very firmly. They also feed on crustaceans and marine worms
and, although they have been persecuted in Scotland by water
bailiffs, young salmon and trout form only a relatively small part of
their diet.

While mergansers spend much of the winter at sea, along the
coasts and estuaries almost anywhere around Britain, and a number
nest along the coast, a significant number of the 2,000 pairs of the
British population fly inland to breed, on the shores of small lochs
and burns in remote Scottish glens. Display is spectacular, with the
male circling the female, the neck down-curved and partially
submerged, and the bill open to show its conspicuous red lining.
As it approaches the female, the neck is straightened, the bird rises

99

in the water, and the wings are opened to display their white patches. The ground nest sites are often in long grass or heather, or among the roots of trees, and are lined with down. The female lays up to twelve eggs, and incubation is by her alone. After hatching, she takes the youngsters to water, where several broods may form a creche.

Cemlyn Bay is also of interest botanically, although as many of the plants grow along the pool edge we did not see them, for fear of disturbing the nesting terns. The plants include the typical shingle ones such as seakale and sea beet, while the bank facing the pool has many salt marsh species – glasswort, sea aster and thrift. Tasselwood, an unusual plant, is found in the pool.

Magor Reserve

Managing body   Gwent Trust for Nature Conservation.
Access   ST 4287. Take bridge over railway line from Magor village. Turn left and park on roadside. Access on foot, eastward. Entrance on right, opposite first pair of semi-detached houses.

Magor Reserve, situated between Caldicot and Newport in Gwent is another of those in which the ornithological interest cannot be isolated from the habitat as a whole. Although comparatively small (about 60 acres), the reserve has an importance far greater than its actual size – containing as it does the last significant area of the original fenland of Gwent, as well as areas of reed-beds, pools, a large pond, woodland, willow carr and some small marshy fields. It is also an example of reen habitat (wetland areas drained by reens or drainage ditches) which is unique to Wales, and it has an impressive list of over 120 water plants and more than 300 species of aquatic invertebrates. Magor was designated an SSSI in 1971.

There are rough footpaths throughout the reserve, and visitors are advised to keep to these, as some of the marshy areas and fens conceal deep water. Wellingtons are essential. Much of the reserve is covered by dense undergrowth where nesting sedge and grasshopper warblers may be seen or heard during spring and summer. The former are frequently parasitised by cuckoos. In the quite extensive reed-beds adjacent to the large man-made pond, reed warblers nest.

Reed warblers are not plentiful in Wales, and those that arrive about the end of April from their winter quarters in Africa, tend to breed in the south-east corner of the country, including Magor. As a species, they are known to nest colonially in reed-beds

(Phragmites) and although the males may be seen displaying – raising the feathers of the crown of the head and flicking the wings and tail – their presence is much more likely to be noticed by the sound of the monotonous, repetitive song, which has been decribed as 'two pebbles being hit together'. The monotony, however, is often broken with bursts of mimicry of other small birds such as chiffchaffs, blue tits and chaffinches. Up to four greenish-white spotted and blotched eggs are laid in June, and for the next three weeks or so either parent may be seen flitting about, as they share both incubation and feeding of the young. Most pairs have two broods, before leaving in August or September for the return flight to tropical Africa – a flight that is interrupted by a stopover in Spain or Portugal.

The pond at Magor and its immediate surroundings (which are overlooked by a fine new hide built by a Manpower Services Commission team in 1981) offer food and nesting sites for coots, mallard, shovelers and little grebes. In 1965 garganeys, which are very rare summer visitors in Wales, actually bred. The marshy fields provide nesting sites for snipe and for yellow wagtails, while along the reeds, moorhens are frequently seen, and the patient watcher may be rewarded with the sight of one of the resident water rails.

The plant life of Magor is very varied, with a number of less common species. Water plants include frogbit, flowering rush and arrowhead, while the fields, some of which are grazed by cattle, support marsh marigold, ragged robin and lesser spearwort. It is Trust policy to continue letting some of the fields to local farmers to prevent them becoming overgrown and reverting to scrub and woodland. Some of the fields which have not been grazed have large areas of sedge species, reed grass, angelica and purple loosestrife, while mare's tail, a rare plant in these parts, grows near the pond.

This is a compact reserve, with something of interest at most times of the year, but it is probably at its best in spring and summer.

Peterstone Wentlooge

Managing body   Gwent Trust for Nature Conservation.
Access   ST 2880. Take A48 east from Cardiff for 5 miles to Castleton. Turn right on minor road through Marshfield to B4239. Park on roadside by T-junction. Path to shore opposite junction.

There is not a great deal to be said about Peterstone Wentlooge reserve in terms of beauty of surroundings, but it is a marvellous

Peterstone Wentlooge on the Severn Estuary is a well-known place for rarities such as the little ringed plover.

place for waders and wildfowl, and for the occasional uncommon species, such as whimbrels, on passage. Situated between Cardiff and Newport, it is a large tract of mud-flats, salt marsh and rough pasture on the Severn Estuary – the estuary itself being of international importance with some ninety to one hundred thousand waders feeding on the mud-flats during winter.

Parking space on the B4239 near the reserve is limited, but permission may be granted by the landlord of the nearby Six Bells public house to use the car-park there. A footpath from the road leads directly to the sea-wall, passing, at its far end, a rectangular basin known as The Gout, into which water drains from the pasture of the surrounding levels. The basin, which then empties through a sluice in the sea-wall is known as a feeding area for local rarities such as wood sandpipers, little stints, ruffs, the occasional avocet and some little ringed plovers.

The best time to visit Peterstone is the two or three hours before high tide, when the rising water brings thousands of waders in to feed near the sea-wall. At any time, however, it is well worth doing as we did – turn right on reaching the wall and walk along on top or immediately below it for about two miles. Wherever we looked there were scores of waders and wildfowl. Great flocks of knots and dunlins (over 4,000 of the latter are recorded as feeding on the mud-flats) flighted up and down the coast, using it as a kind of avian highway. Oystercatchers were there, being their usual talkative selves, while curlews stalked around the mud-flats, probing for food. Every so often, a group would take to the air, uttering their wonderful call. We saw a few grey plovers, but in spite of careful searching, we did not find any greenshanks.

Redshanks were there in plenty – their diagnostic 'three white triangles' (the white markings on rump and trailing edges of the wings) making identification simple, even on the rare occasions when they were silent in flight. In spite of their maddening habit of alerting everything in the area to the presence of even the stealthiest of birdwatchers, we would miss their presence if they disappeared from our coastal habitats. Of course, the shore line is quieter in the breeding season when large flocks of these delightful birds move inland to nesting sites – but at Peterstone, some stay to nest on the reserve. The courtship displays are elaborate, the male establishing a territory and then performing a special flight accompanied by song to attract a mate. He rises up into the air with very rapidly beating wings, then glides slowly down again to stand, head held high with outstretched but downwardly curved wings and fanned tail. The female lays four spotted buff-coloured eggs in a grass-lined nest concealed in a tussock, and, as soon as the chicks are hatched, they leave the nest, encouraged by calls from the parents. There are recorded instances of parent redshanks moving their young to safer places by carrying them between their thighs.

As well as the waders at Peterstone, we saw plenty of ducks – shelducks, which breed on the reserve, quite a number of shovelers, for which Peterstone is one of the most important sites in Wales, and plenty of mallard. Other species recorded there include the pintail, scaup, scoter, long-tailed duck, garganey and gadwall. As we walked along the sea-wall we kept an eye on the Levels inland, and saw some fieldfares and thrushes, but no redwings, nor even a glimpse of the short-eared owls which quarter the flat pastures in search of prey.

Gelli-Hir Wood

Managing body   Glamorgan Naturalists' Trust.
Access   SS 5692. Take B4271 out of Swansea. Turn right to Cilonnen, and reserve entrance is on right several yards down. Park on verge.

For lovers of deep woodland, this little reserve should not be missed. Situated on the Gower Peninsula, it is a remnant of the dense woodland that once covered the area before it was cleared for grazing. There are pathways throughout the wood and a stroll down any of these is a delight – but wellingtons are advisable in all but the driest summer, as some of it is rather boggy. Much of the

103

wood is of quite dense oak – some really fine specimens – and in the drier, slightly higher sections in the north-west corner, ash, wych elm, beech, hazel and lime are present.

There is a stream running through the wood, and several pools, surrounded and lined by typical wetland trees such as alder and willow. The largest pool is in deep woodland, and indeed could quite easily be missed, but it is worth finding, as it is rich in wetland plants such as bulrush, wild angelica, bur-reed, golden saxifrage and water-plantain. It provides perfect nesting for mallard and teal, both of which we saw.

There are plenty of woodland birds, such as tree-creepers and tits, while sparrow-hawks and tawny owls breed. As we made our way along a path near the edge of the wood, we surprised a buzzard, apparently feeding on the ground in an area of rough grassland just outside the reserve fence. These birds, too, are said to breed in Gelli-Hir.

In addition to the birds, the reserve is renowned for insects and butterflies – such as the comma, holly blue and silver-washed fritillary. The latter is interesting as it feeds on marsh violets in this reserve, instead of the more customary heath dog violet.

Dinas RSPB Reserve

Managing body   RSPB.
Access   SN 7947. On Llandovery – Llyn Brianne road, north of Rhandirmwyn.
Other information   Visitor centre and car-park. Trail. Open all year.

This spectacular and beautiful Welsh reserve is in red kite country – and for us it was one of the most frustrating days we have spent! The reserve consists principally of Dinas Hill, around which there is a clearly defined path. A word of warning though – some of the steeper, rock-strewn sections of the trail around Dinas do require a certain degree of agility, but it is well worth it for those who can manage it. Dinas is part of the Gwenffrwd reserve, described in another chapter, but in spite of its towering cliffs and rocky gorge, it is set in much softer country than its near neighbour.

A visit to the reception centre established that a kite had been seen several times during the previous three days, so we set off in high hopes that we might see our first one. But although we saw plenty of woodland birds during our circuit of the hill – we had neither sight nor sound of a red kite. It was maddening to return to the car-park some hours later to learn that someone had just seen one on the far side of the hill.

The trail starts in a corner of the car-park and leads, by means of a wooden boardwalk, for about 500 yards through a woodland of mixed oak, hazel and alder carr, across a section of boggy ground and beside an attractive stream. We saw a number of tits, including a twittering party of long-tailed, and one or two tree-creepers, and along the margins of the stream we saw a grey and a pied wagtail.

At the end of the boardwalk the trail, which encircles the hill, branches off in two directions. We chose the left and walked along the well-defined path through a predominantly oak wood, and were delighted to see pied flycatchers, nuthatches, a variety of tits and several willow warblers. Also recorded in the woods are wood warblers and tree pipits. We saw a number of redstarts – including two youngsters, rather charmingly sitting side by side on a fence while their parents visited them from time to time with insects and tiny worms.

Dinas, with its rushing stream set in the Welsh hills, is a typical habitat for the grey wagtail.

The male redstart is a handsome bird in full breeding plumage, with bright chestnut-red tail, rump and breast, black throat, white forehead and grey back. The female is duller overall, except for her tail – the latter being flicked up and down constantly by both sexes. The males arrive from north-west Africa in April and take up their breeding territories, using the higher branches of trees as song posts. When the female arrives a little later, the male makes effective use of his bright coloration – bowing with drooped wings, outstretched head and neck and widely fanned tail in a spirited display, which is followed by an equally spirited chase from perch to perch in the tree canopy. Redstarts like to nest in a hole or crevice, frequently using holes in tree trunks or cavities in stone walls for their bark and grass nest, which is lined with hair and feathers and is built by the female. She lays up to eight pale blue eggs. Frequently two broods of the heavily speckled and mottled young are reared before all join the flight back to Africa in August.

About half-way round the hill we began to hear the sound of rushing water, and the trail started to climb quite steeply. The terrain became much more rocky – the boulders encrusted with lichens and mosses and ferns growing out of the crevices – and we looked down from what had become a very steep-sided valley into the fast-moving river below. It was a spectacular view, with the white water rushing through a narrow rock-strewn gorge. The hillside was covered with small, stunted oaks, and although we could hear no bird-song above the roar of the water, the various woodland birds were everywhere. However, we searched in vain for the stock doves which breed in the high crags above the river.

After some quite testing clambering over the rocks and gnarled tree trunks, the path began to descend, and soon we came down into the open valley, where the river widens out and flows rather more gently, but against the background of yet another rock-faced hill. Nestling in grassy areas were large patches of orchids, and, a little further downstream in some marshy ground, was a bright splash of colour provided by a stand of yellow flags. A heron stood statuesquely on a rock in the shallows, and further down again a dipper bobbed up and down. Goosanders have also been seen in some of the rock-pools.

We wandered back to where the track met the boardwalk and returned to the car-park – disappointed that we had not seen a kite, but thoroughly delighted with the number of woodland birds, the mosses, the lichens, the ferns, and, of course, with the lovely scenery of this part of Wales.

Gwenffrwd RSPB Reserve

Managing body   RSPB.
Access   SN 7546. Off minor road to Rhandirmwyn from Llandovery or
Pumpsaint.
Other information   Trail guide from the reception centre. Open Easter –
August, Monday and Wednesday only.

It is possible on this reserve to see ravens, red kites, peregrines,
merlins and buzzards – but it is much more likely that the latter will
be the only one of the five on view. Gwenffrwd, however, is a
reserve that it is a pleasure to visit for the scenery alone, even in the
unlikely event of not seeing a single interesting bird from start to
finish.

A trail guide, available from the visitor centre and shop, is a
prerequisite to setting out on the four mile walk. It is full of
information and gives the visitor a useful understanding of the
structure and ecology of the reserve, and of some of the
management techniques. It also draws attention to former
mismanagement of this and other upland tracts of Wales and of
British uplands as a whole. The guide does warn the walker that the
path is, in places, damp, and more than a little stony, and
personally, I found the steep road down the far side of the valley
very hard walking indeed.

We followed the orange trail markers from the centre and soon
struck off across fields towards the river valley, which is quite
thickly wooded. In the birch trees, which we came to first, were
some nest boxes and, as requested, we left them well alone. The
leaflet told us that about a third of them would be used by pied
flycatchers, and another third by tits. As we went deeper into the
wood towards the river (the Gwenffrwd), the trees became more
varied and included hazel, ash and oak, and, right beside the river
itself, some alder.

We saw a great spotted woodpecker, a couple of tree-creepers, a
willow warbler, a coal tit, one or two spotted flycatchers and a
mallard. Other birds known to be in the wood include marsh tits,
nuthatches (which we could hear but could not locate) and wood
warblers. We crossed the river by the bridge, and although it
seemed likely dipper territory, we did not see any on this occasion.
In this sheltered valley it was quite warm, and several dragonflies
were hawking up and down the river, and a couple of damselflies
were hovering around the marshy parts. Those known to be on the
reserve include the demoiselle agrion and golden ring dragonfly.

As we crossed the field, the mountain that we were to climb

107

towered over us, and it looked as if we might be in for a strenuous day. We came to a hedge-lined lane – the hedge providing nesting for long-tailed tits, robins and dunnocks. Pied flycatchers, tree pipits and redstarts bring their young from the wood to the hedgerows, where they shelter while the parents look for food.

The lane led up to a farmhouse and outbuildings, and, threading our way through the yard, we looked carefully at an old hollow oak tree which dominated the top end. The guide told us that it was probably over 300 years old, and thus likely to be one of the old native forest trees. What changes it has seen in the landscape over its lifetime!

From the yard, the track climbed steadily upwards along the side of the hill through gorse and bracken growing between the shaley rock. The first feature of special interest we came to was a small hanging oakwood, clinging to the side of the mountain rather precariously, rooted as it is in a very thin layer of soil. Because of this, the trees are stunted and gnarled, but still provide niches for nest boxes to attract pied flycatchers. They also provide anchorage for mosses, lichens and the very attractive common polypody fern. This piece of woodland has been neglected, and continual grazing in and around it has resulted in a lack of regeneration, and also a lack of understorey. Now the RSPB management plan is to curtail grazing in order to encourage regeneration and provide a more suitable environment for birds, such as wood warblers.

The track continued upwards, and just before we reached a rough, stony road our attention was drawn to two kinds of tree-planting which have taken place since the reserve was acquired in 1967. Above us, single trees had been planted among the bracken over a period of time, with the idea of spreading the damage caused by grazing sheep, while in a fenced enclosure below us, trees were planted densely all at the same time. At this stage, we paused to look back across the valley, and enjoyed the varying greens of the hills as the sunlight and clouds made dappled patterns on them – one minute the hanging oakwood we had just been in looked green and lush, and the next, as the cloud blotted out the sun, it appeared almost black and cheerless.

From this point the rough track took us right up through heather moorland to a hide – *en route* we saw numbers of meadow pipits, whinchats and wheatears. We turned off to the right and followed the markers to the only hide on the reserve. As we went in, the wind from which we had been protected hitherto, whistled around us – and we noted without any surprise the strong wires mooring the building firmly to the ground. When we opened the flaps we saw just how exposed it was – perched on the top of a mountain –

Gwenffrwd is the perfect place for birds of the wild uplands, such as red kites, buzzards (seen here) and ravens.

and how different was the scenery now spread out in front and below us. It was wild, remote, exciting and very beautiful, as range after range of the Cambrian mountains stretched away into the distance. It seemed the perfect place for birds of the wild uplands, such as red kites, buzzards and ravens, and it was not long before we spotted a buzzard.

The guide drew our attention to the relative lack of heather moorland among the high tops, and pointed out that the heavy sheep grazing has resulted in many of the hills being turned over to unpalatable grasslands, with over-burning and over-grazing encouraging the spread of bracken. So much of the land having now become unpalatable for sheep, there is real danger of it being taken over for forestry, and neither that, nor the grassland with bracken, is attractive to two birds in particular which used to live in these parts – the red grouse and the merlin. As the guide points out, there are now fewer pairs of merlins breeding in Wales than red kites.

From the hide we re-traced our steps down the hill to the track, and began the steep descent down the far side of the valley. The trail guide explained that most of the area would have been covered with trees until about 3,000 years ago – with birch and some Scots pine on the tops, and ash, elm, oak, alder and hazel lower down. Then wandering tribes of men moved across the country, foraging for food and making small clearances in the woods. With the coming of metal implements, a more settled agricultural economy began, and the men began to make larger clearances of wood from the valleys, and introduced the field system. Further clearance occurred in the uplands, where stock was grazed in the summer. By about the beginning of the seventeenth century, it is thought that nearly half the natural woodlands of Wales had been destroyed, although the valuable oak woods of the valley sides were often spared. These were subject to a form of management to encourage regeneration until the beginning of this century. Then, the economic products of the oak woods, charcoal and timber, declined, and management all but ceased. The consequent unlimited grazing and widespread felling since then has left vast areas of the country with sparse tree cover – with the obvious implications for birds and other wildlife.

Quite near the bottom of the road, we came to a place where a mountain stream comes tumbling over a waterfall and although it was dry at the time, in winter it crosses the road and goes over a man-made waterfall. The rocks hereabout are covered with mosses and lichens, and we found an example of Wilson's filmy fern – a fern typical of the spray zone of waterfalls in the area. From there, we followed the trail back to the car-park – having thoroughly enjoyed an interesting and very instructive walk in superb surroundings.

Castle Woods

Managing body   West Wales Naturalists' Trust.
Access   SN 6322. Take Carmarthen road (A40) from Llandeilo town centre. On right by ambulance station is a car-park. Reserve reached through public park opposite.

A visit to the Castle Woods reserve, managed by the West Wales Naturalists' Trust, gave us the opportunity of a delightful walk through the Dynevor Deer Park to the woods themselves. Approached by way of Penlan Park on the outskirts of Llandeilo, the deer park is set in undulating and, at times, quite steep countryside, made all the more attractive by small groups of trees, including sweet chestnut, lime and conifers. A herd of fallow deer, of which we saw some signs, and a few red deer roam the park; there are a number of badger setts, and otters have been seen along the nearby river. Within the park, the West Wales Naturalists' nature trail, marked by badger footprint signs, leads around the edges of the fields close to the water-meadows where wetland birds congregate in winter, and, eventually, up to the entrance to the woods.

The woods cling to a very steep limestone escarpment overlooking the River Twyi, and afford some magnificent views. Entering the gate, there is a plantation of conifers on the right and a deciduous woodland on the left, with oak, ash, and some wych elm – a piece of woodland thought to be part of the ancient primary forest of West Wales. There are also a number of other species including beech, cherry, holly and box.

The woods have a rich variety of birds, with all three woodpeckers (we saw both great and lesser spotteds), goldcrests and long-tailed, marsh and coal tits. Tree-creepers were much in evidence, and we heard a nuthatch tapping away long before a careful search revealed it. It was relatively early in the summer, but we saw a blackthroat, a chiffchaff, a couple of pied flycatchers and a redstart. Garden warblers and whitethroats are also recorded on the reserve.

We followed the broad road right up to the now ruined Dynevor Castle, and then took the much narrower and somewhat overgrown track behind it, following it for some way down the hill, where we met yet another party – quite a large one this time – of

Castle Woods cling to a very steep limestone escarpment overlooking the River Twyi, and have a rich variety of birds.

long-tailed tits. The delicate colouring of these lovely little birds make them a great favourite, and it is always a pleasure to hear the distinctive twittering that always accompanies their forays through the trees and bushes. One of the most interesting features about them is their beautifully constructed domed nests, built in the fork of a tree or in a gorse bush, and which they may start building as early as February, taking over two weeks to complete the elaborate structures. They are painstakingly constructed from moss, held together with cobwebs and hair, and covered with lichen if this is available or, in cities, even with paper or polystyrene. The interior is lined with feathers, and the incredible total of 2,000 feather-collecting journeys have been recorded in the construction of a single nest.

Long-tailed tits have an interesting method of dealing with hard items of food: they hang from a twig with one foot, and hold the piece of food in the other while pecking at it with their deep yet narrow bill – a bill ideally shaped to enable them to extract insects from narrow crevices. They are a species that clearly believes in co-operation. Being exceptionally vulnerable to hard weather, several families will roost together for warmth, often in a compact ball, with their long tails sticking out. In the summer, when the young are being reared, parents whose nesting has failed, will often help to feed another pair's youngsters.

Apart from the birds, Castle Wood has a splendid variety of plants, and is particularly rich in lichens. The rare tree lungwort, which only grows in areas with exceptionally clean air, is found. Toothwort – found in only two other stations in the county – is also present.

Penderi Reserve

Managing body   West Wales Naturalists' Trust.
Access   SN 5573. 5 miles south of Aberystwyth on A487. Access through Pen-y-Graig farm.

The Penderi Reserve on the coast south of Aberystwyth is traversed by the Coastal Footpath, but is approached through Pen-y-Graig farm on the A487 road. Anyone not able to negotiate fields with a gradient that often seemed like one in two should avoid this one – but for the strong-legged it is certainly worth the struggle!

The reserve is noted for its hanging oak woods which, sited as they are right on the very edge of the cliffs, may reasonably be described as more hanging than most. They are fenced off, and it really is not advisable to enter them. However, looking down on them, one can see a few small woodland birds among the tree-tops.

The sea-birds are the greatest points of interest, and on the very high, steep and crumbly cliffs, there are breeding colonies of shags,

Fulmars winged their way along the coast, just a few feet away from us on the cliff-tops.

cormorants, fulmars and herring gulls. Ravens and choughs have also been seen along this rugged stretch of coastline. We had excellent views of both shags and cormorants, sitting somewhat morosely on the cliff ledges, while fulmars and herring gulls floated past, just a few feet away from us along the cliff-tops.

We were particularly fascinated and rather alarmed by the sheep that leapt up and down the almost sheer cliff-faces with extraordinary agility. They seemed to think nothing of standing on tiny little pinnacles of rock – all four feet crammed onto what seemed totally inadequate space, with no room for manoeuvre at all.

We spent an instructive time sitting on the cliff edge making sure we could distinguish between shags and cormorants – not always easy at a distance. Shags are, on average, about six inches shorter than cormorants and rather slimmer. In flight, the former has a rather quicker wing beat. Both, when perching, may extend the wings, but the shags' are, as a rule, held straighter. In summer, the adult cormorant shows white patches on face and flank; the shag has a yellow gape, which is not so noticeable. In the water, the cormorant has a distinctive way of pointing its beak upwards, while the shag's beak is held at less of an angle, and is slimmer in outline. Another distinction is that the shag has twelve tail feathers, whereas the cormorant has fourteen – a feature unlikely to be noticed except at unusually close quarters!

Ynys-Hir RSPB Reserve

Managing body   RSPB.
Access   SN 6896. On north side of A487 Aberystwyth – Machynlleth road in Furnace village.
Other information   Reception Centre. Leaflet. Open April – September certain days only.

There can be few reserves of its size in Britain that have such a variety of habitats as Ynys-Hir on the Dyfi Estuary in North Wales. Within its 630 acres there is the estuary itself, salt marshes and mud-flats, farm pasture, broad-leaved and coniferous woodland, marshlands, a bog, a stream, a deep gorge, rocky outcrops and a rocky bracken-clad hill overlooking the rest of the reserve from the southern side of the Aberystwyth to Machynlleth road. The reserve is thus in two sections, with the visitor centre being on the northern side of the main road, and approached through a gateway in Furnace village.

Looking across the salt marshes to the estuary, where a range of waders and wildfowl feed and roost.

From the visitor centre, we joined one of the nature trails leading into the beautiful ancient oak wood which was absolutely filled with bird-song and calls. The wood supports the greater proportion of the reserve's breeding species (of which there are nearly seventy) and nest boxes have been placed to encourage them. We saw a pied flycatcher, several spotted woodpeckers were about, and jays made their presence known by their customary noisy exchanges. We glimpsed the male of a pair of kestrels that were nesting. At night, tawny owls (another nesting species) are heard.

Of the nine warblers breeding at Ynys-Hir, we saw several blackcaps and willow warblers, a chiffchaff and a wood warbler. Also in the woods, were a variety of tits and nuthatches – all making use of some of the nest boxes. I do not know if there has been an increase in the numbers of tree-creepers recently, but we have seen them in so many places – and Ynys-Hir was no exception. They are such charming little birds – sometimes being likened to mice as they scurry up and around the trunks of trees, their stiff tails pressed hard against the bark for support. Their needle-sharp curved beaks are ideal for extracting insects, spiders and larvae from crevices in and under bark. Crevices often provide nesting sites, as do the cramped spaces behind loose bark, or dense curtain of ivy. Mating is preceded by a courtship display which includes chases, a fluttering flight and wing-shivering. It is followed by nest-building by both birds, although incubation is done largely by the female. Two broods are common.

We followed the steep pathway down the side of the hill to more level ground where the track led towards the estuary. Here, at high tide, a range of waders – oystercatchers, redshanks, curlews and dunlins – and, in winter, wildfowl such as wigeons, goldeneyes, mergansers, tufteds, shovelers, mallard and teal are present in some numbers. In the marshy area, with its reed-beds, grasshopper warblers and reed warblers are present, as are reed buntings and a number of snipe. A flock of Greenland white-fronted geese (the most southerly flock in Britain) sometimes visits the reserve's section of the estuary from their more usual feeding grounds just to the west. As might be expected, raptors are often present and, particularly in winter, peregrines, hen harriers and merlins are seen. Occasionally, in spring and summer, a red kite is recorded.

On our way to one of the hides overlooking the salt marshes, we saw quite a collection of redstarts in a group of oak trees along the edge of some of the farmland. These birds are relatively common at Ynys-Hir, some nesting in the boxes provided. There was not a great deal to be seen from the salt marsh hide, and as the Heronry Hide was closed to avoid disturbing the nesting birds, we did not venture onto that part of the reserve. For the same reason, we missed seeing the River Einion which runs along the border of the reserve. It is, however, a good place for birds, with common sandpipers, mergansers, dippers and grey wagtails all recorded.

Before returning to the car-park, we visited the tree-top hide in the oak wood, from where we had an extremely close view of some of the passerines flitting about in the top of the canopy. We then moved on to the section of the reserve on the opposite side of the road, Foel Fawr. Here, a selection of paths lead up the hillside – a typical moorland area with bracken and heath and a variety of heathland birds such as yellowhammers, wheatears, stonechats and meadow pipits. In the evenings, nightjars are heard. Best of all, however, was the glorious view looking back over the rest of the reserve, and right across the estuary with Snowdonia in the background.

Cors Caron
National Nature Reserve

Managing body   NCC.
Access   SN 7063. Take A485 from Lampeter to Tregaron, then B4343 towards Pontrhydfendigaid. Park in lay-by.
Other information   Permit for all but Railway Walk, from Warden: Menawel, Ffair Rhos, Pontrhydfendigaid, Ystrad Meurig, Dyfed.

Cors Caron in Dyfed is a classic raised bog, and, with its enormous variety of bog and water plants, it is a place of absolute delight to botanists. Ornithologists too, find it very rewarding, as it has a long list of recorded species. To us it is rather special, as it was here that at last we saw our very first red kite.

There is free and unrestricted access to the edge of the reserve along the Old Railway Walk (for which a descriptive leaflet is obtainable in a dispenser near the entrance). To go across the bog itself, a permit from the warden is required, and it is certainly worth it, as so much more can be seen and enjoyed. But, great care should be taken, if walking across the bog, to keep to the trodden paths, as the surface is treacherous in places. The warning notice placed near a wooden boardwalk giving access to non-permit holders to see the bog at close quarters is graphic and should be observed!

The Old Railway Walk leads, as the name suggests, along the path of a disused railway, and although never flooded or impassable, it is not very pleasant walking due to the remains of the stone ballast. But it does give a good idea of the bog, and from it much of interest may be seen.

The walk took us first into a shallow cutting with scrub and small trees on either side, consisting of willow, blackthorn, ash, hawthorn and some hazel – all growing rather more vigorously than elsewhere in the reserve because of the nutrients and lime released into the soil from materials used in the construction of the railway. Among this scrub and in some of the young trees we saw a variety of passerines, such as willow warblers and blackcaps, together with the usual wrens and robins, which feed and nest in the area. A number of magpies were also about, and they, too, nest in the blackthorn.

An interesting point was made in the leaflet concerning the greater tussock sedge which was growing near a clump of willows by the bog-edge, and which was visible from the trail. The dry foliage of this plant was formerly used for making hassocks for the local churches and chapels.

It was a warm but overcast day, and as we walked along we saw a number of butterflies – common blue and small heath – and several common lizards. We noticed where, as the leaflet described, trees and shrubs had been cut back at various points as part of the management programme to create a mixed woodland and scrub, thus encouraging as wide a range of wildlife as possible. A little further along and to our right was a farm, and near the track a very thick, dense area of nettles and thistles. These have grown up as a result of various nutrients seeping from the farm, and the seeds provide winter food for the smaller birds.

From there the track crossed the bog, thus giving us good views, and we heard several curlews calling. From time to time one or two got up, calling as they went. It was past the peak of the breeding season, so we did not hear any snipe drumming, but we put up one or two later on when we were right out on the bog. A group of alders by the track provide cover and nest sites for willow warblers, several of which we heard and we also heard a grasshopper warbler. During the course of the walk we saw several kestrels out over the bog, and two buzzards, but the other predators, such as sparrow-hawks, did not put in an appearance. Merlins and peregrines are sometimes seen on passage in spring and autumn, while hen harriers are present during the winter. Both barn and short-eared owls may be seen hunting over the bog at dawn and dusk.

We soon came to a small gate on the left of the path which opened onto a section of boardwalk, allowing a good look at the surface of the bog. Typical bog plants were there, such as purple moor grass, sphagnum moss (of various species), ling, heather and sundew – the latter in flower.

At the end of the walk, we came to the impressive observation tower, set high on pillars and approached by a ladder. It gave wide views out over the bog, and at the back, looked right up into the mountains. From it, we could see where the Afon Fflur river joined the Afon Teifi, and where, at certain times, dippers are seen. Otters have also been seen from the tower, if the entries in the visitors' record book are to be believed. Certainly otters have been reliably reported over the years, they probably feed on the many eels in the rivers. Migrant salmon and trout also come up the rivers to spawn.

In front of the hide, a scrape and pool have been excavated, but we saw nothing much there other than some mallard; at various times an assortment of both waders and wildfowl has been seen. Teal and wigeons winter on the reserve, and also a number of whoopers, attracted by the open water of the rivers; while among the waders, curlews, redshanks and snipe are the most common. Golden plovers, ruffs, spotted redshanks, dunlins and whimbrels are recorded as passage migrants or winter visitors. Water rails, moorhens and coots are all present throughout the year.

Armed with our permits, we set out across the bog, or rather, on the firmer ground surrounding and intersecting the bog. A number of painted posts helped us follow the firm ground, and we soon reached the river, which floods widely in winter. This waterway is very attractive, with great expanses of yellow waterlilies at a number of points. As we went further away from the walk, we saw more and more curlews, and also a number of meadow pipits and a pied wagtail hopping about in one of the dried-out areas of sphagnum. Several pairs of mallard were on the river, and they took off in a great flurry as we approached, only to land again several hundred yards ahead of us, repeating the exercise as we followed

Among the passage and winter migrants seen at Cors Caron are golden plovers.

the river. It winds through the bog, and is crossed at different points by small bridges.

We were the only people out on the bog that day, and there was a wonderful feeling of solitude and remoteness. We did hope we might see a kite, but our luck seemed to be out. We decided to return to the Railway Walk where we had parked the car, and go out on the south-east bog. A really fascinating educational booklet is available from the warden about this area of the reserve; it is for the real enthusiast and is quite technical in places, having been prepared by the Nature Conservancy Council and the University College of Wales at Aberystwyth. It follows in some detail an educational trail across the bog, describing the botanical and historical development of the habitats. Much of this trail is on wooden boardwalks, and it is very important that visitors should not stray from them – partly because of the damage that could be done to the bog, and partly because it can be very dangerous.

It was while we were engaged in following this trail that we saw – at last – a red kite! We were examining some of the bog plants when we happened to look up, and there it was, flapping majestically away from us – glinting gold in the weak sunlight, its deeply forked tail and white wing patches clearly visible, leaving no doubt at all about its identification. It flew on, finally disappearing behind some trees in the distance, leaving us absolutely delighted.

It is encouraging that these magnificent birds seem to be on the increase in Wales. A number of people will probably have seen the film of some of them on the BBC's *Blue Peter* programme, where they were shown scavenging on a rubbish tip not very far from Cors Caron. It is strange to think that the streets of London were once one of their principal habitats.

While we were out on this part of the bog we examined a number of 'flashes' or permanent shallow backwaters which act as a refuge for over-wintering birds. At this time, because of an exceptionally dry summer, most of them were almost dried out, but we firmly resisted the temptation to walk into the middle of them to examine them more closely, as the mud can be treacherous. After the flooding of autumn and winter, these flashes form a valuable food source for birds, who feed on the seeds of many of the aquatic plants which are left stranded near the outer margins as the waters recede.

Northern England

South Walney Nature Reserve

Managing body   Cumbria Trust for Nature Conservation.
Access   SD 2162. From Barrow-in-Furness cross bridge to Isle of Walney.
Turn left at traffic lights and follow Promenade and Ocean Road. Take fourth
turning on left (Carr Lane) and continue for 5 miles – the last mile or so is
very rough.
Other information   Parking at Coastguard Cottages. Illustrated booklet
from warden.

South Walney, managed by the Cumbria Trust for Nature
Conservation, has a special place in the annals of natural history as
the site chosen by Professor Niko Tinbergen of the Animal
Behaviour Research Group at Oxford University for his famous
work on the behaviour of gulls. The reserve featured in the book
Signals for Survival by Professor Tinbergen, Hugh Falkus and Eric
Ennion, and in the film of the same title by the two first-named.
Before exploring the reserve, it is necessary to buy a permit – a
mere formality which can be overcome, in the absence of the
warden, by putting the appropriate small fee in the 'honesty box'.

The crescent-shaped island of South Walney, about ten miles
long and three-quarters of a mile across at its widest, is the largest of
seven off the tip of the Furness Peninsula. It is low and windswept,
with its western shore facing into the Irish sea. Having negotiated
the five or six miles from Barrow-in-Furness and the very bumpy
gravel road for the last mile or so, the visitor's first sight of the
reserve may be, depending on the state of the tide, the extensive
mud-flats bordering the island's eastern shore facing Barrow
Harbour. These provide rich feeding grounds for a variety of
waders and sea-birds.

Although the two immense gull colonies (herring and black-
backed) are of great importance, South Walney has many
interesting features within its 230 acres. Basically, it is a dune-
covered shingle spit, but it includes, in addition to the mud-flats
already mentioned, salt marshes, sand and shingle beaches, and
both fresh and brackish pools – supporting an exceedingly varied
flora and fauna.

There are two nature trails around the reserve, and they are worth following, not just from the point of view of interest, but because they lead the visitor carefully round so as not to disturb the nesting birds or to interrupt any research that may be going on.

We set off on the red trail, which is three miles long, and the first stopping place was the Observation Hide not far from the car-park and the warden's cottage. Here, in the building adapted from a World War II generator house, its walls lined with pictures and information about *Signals for Survival* we looked out over a section of the gulls' breeding grounds on the grass-covered dunes.

The gullery occupies the greater part of the reserve, and has grown enormously from just a few nesting pairs in the 1920s to approximately 20,000 pairs of each of the two main species. Not for nothing does the trail guide warn visitors to wear strong head covering as a protection against the aggressive gulls if they happen to go near the gullery in the nesting season! The gullery has expanded almost to the limits of the available space, and although the nesting of the two species does overlap to a small degree, the lesser black-backs prefer the western end of the reserve among the bracken and the grass-lined valleys, while their herring gull neighbours tend to congregate more on the turf and marram-covered dunes at the eastern end. In the areas which are common to both, the lesser black-backs opt for the lower ground of the valley bottoms and the lower slopes of the dunes, while the herrings choose the higher ground. Even though they are closely related and nest in such close proximity, inter-breeding is extremely rare, and this is believed to be due to the chicks early imprinting on their parents. Herring gull chicks are thought to recognise their parents chiefly by the yellow eye-ring and grey back, while the black-backed chicks are believed to imprint on the scarlet eye-ring and dark back coloration.

At the time of our visit in early April, the migratory lesser black-backed gulls were returning from their winter quarters in the Iberian Peninsula and North Africa. They were beginning to establish their territories, sometimes among the resident herring gulls, only a comparatively small number of which winter away from Walney. Our early visit meant that there were few, if any, nests, but courtship was in progress, and there was a great deal of noisy calling and a certain amount of territorial squabbling.

Leaving the hide, we walked westwards through some of the black-backed gullery, and, as the tide was quite high, we kept down below the bank fringing the shingle beach, so as not to disturb the many eiders which the warden had told us would be coming ashore at that time. We skirted the line of saline pools behind the bank. (This is where the two nature trails divide – the blue trail

In early April, the migratory lesser black-backed gulls return from their winter quarters in the Iberian Peninsula and North Africa.

being, in effect, a short-cut through the dunes to the Irish Sea side of the reserve.) Gulls of both species were very much in evidence, and also on the pools were mallard and a few redshanks, fossicking around in the shallows.

The pools are in an area of the island which, at the turn of the century, was the site of extensive salt extraction. This proved uneconomic, and the remains of the buildings used in the industry are an unsightly reminder of the failure. Gravel extraction took its place, and the pools and the bay between the spit and the main island are its visible signs – so it can be said to have benefited the birds. Working of the gravel deposits is still in progress today.

Although we had seen a number of eiders off shore when the tide was out, we were certainly not prepared for the sight that greeted us when we crawled up the bank and peered over. There, roosting on the shingle and in great rafts on the water, were hundreds of eider ducks and drakes. Although eiders are now one of the most numerous ducks in the world (the European population alone is estimated at about two million), to see so many in one place and at such close quarters was a memorable experience. The numbers on the South Walney Reserve have increased considerably over the last twenty years, and it is now one of the most important breeding grounds – grounds which, although at present restricted to Scotland, Northumberland and Cumbria, are gradually extending further south.

Eiders are almost exclusively sea ducks, so the courtship and mating takes place on the water, with much head bobbing and the slightly comical 'plum-in-the-mouth' cooing of the males. The males can become very aggressive to rivals, chasing them off – their speed through the water being increased by the use of their wings as paddles. At South Walney, the eider ducks come ashore to nest, laying a clutch of six or seven greenish eggs in a nest which is lined with – naturally – eider down. Eider ducks are well known for their tenacity when sitting, and will even allow themselves to be approached quite closely. They leave their eggs for just a few minutes a day for food and water. When the ducklings hatch, after a month's incubation, their mother takes them down to the water as soon as they are dry, where they often join the rafts of adults and other young. According to observations made at South Walney, the duck is unique among the others breeding on the reserve (such as mallard and shelduck) in her method of defending her young from falling prey to marauding gulls. Instead of the youngsters scattering and becoming easy prey, they cluster round their mother who fends off the attacking gulls with her bill.

After watching the eiders for some time, we moved round the point and into the Pier Hide, which overlooks Lighthouse Bay (the one made by the salt extractors) and across to the spit. In the bay were more eiders, some shelducks and a small number of redshanks. At other times of the year waders such as bar-tailed godwits, knots, dunlins and turnstones may be seen here or on the spit, as well as on the mud-flats and the shingle beaches in other parts of the reserve. The bay contains a well-developed salt marsh with typical plants such as the glassworts, thrift and spartina grass.

The spit is a sand and shingle outcrop on the eastern end of the island, and in addition to being a refuge for large numbers of waders in the winter, it is the site of the tern breeding colonies. Consequently it is 'out-of-bounds' to visitors for two hours before and after high tide, and at all times from 1 April to 30 August. Arctic, common, little and Sandwich terns all nest in this area, returning in April from their long migration. The spit also has a black-headed gull colony.

From the pier we went past the Lighthouse to post eight, where a short green trail led us to the Groyne Hide on the southerly tip of the island. Here we saw several more terns and also a number of gannets winging their way along the coastline. The hide is an excellent viewing point for the guillimots, scoters, skuas, fulmars and shearwaters that pass by but rarely, if ever, come ashore. In stormy times a number of rarities have been recorded.

We re-joined the main blue trail, which led us along a shallow, turf-lined valley between two rows of marram-covered dunes – and

Eider ducks are well known for their tenacity when sitting, and will even allow themselves to be approached quite closely.

it was here that we were surrounded by gulls. They were everywhere – in the sky, on the ground, whistling round our heads, calling and screaming abuse! We were lucky, none of them actually attacked us – in marked contrast to some visitors who have had to leave the gullery under concentrated mobbing by these aggressive birds. None the less, we did get a good idea of what it must be like at the height of the nesting season.

Some distance further on we came to the Sea Hide, which faces out towards the Welsh coast, and from which more passing sea-birds and divers are frequently seen. From there we went on to the penultimate post on the trail, the Heligoland Trap, used to catch migrating birds for ringing. The principal aim is to study the west coast migration patterns, and the age, population and distribution of various species. Some rarities have been caught in the trap over the years, including an American white-throated sparrow twenty years ago, and a paddyfield warbler in 1982.

The last stage of the trail, post fourteen, is the freshwater Gate

Pond, around which many of the eiders nest. The pond and its surrounding vegetation provide food for moorhens, snipe, and wildfowl such as wigeons and teal. From here, we returned to the car-park, pausing on our way to watch some ringed plovers on the mud-flats which were being revealed once more by the receding tide.

This is super reserve – and although we concentrated on the birds, its varied habitats offer plenty of interest for the all-round naturalist. All these are described in a well-produced booklet available from the warden at an exceptionally reasonable price.

St Bees Head RSPB Reserve

Managing body   RSPB.
Access   NX 9612. St Bees Beach car-park. Cars must not be driven up the private road to cliffs at Sandwith.

The first thing to be said about this reserve is that it should not be tackled by those whose head for heights is suspect, nor by anyone who is unable to cope with some quite steep gradients. But, with those provisos, it is a reserve that is well worth the considerable effort, offering some spectacular and colourful coastal scenery. It is one of the largest sea-bird sites on the west coast of England, and its 300 feet high pink sandstone cliffs offer plenty of nesting ledges.

From the car-park at St Bees, we climbed steeply up the path to the cliff-top and set off on the two and a half mile walk to the North Head Lighthouse. Almost immediately, we saw a variety of sea-birds flying past – herring gulls, kittiwakes, fulmars and the occasional cormorant flying low over the water. The vegetation on the cliff-tops is basically a mixture of gorse, heather and grassland, and we saw stonechats and several wheatears in among the bushes.

There is a fence along some of the cliff edge, but under no circumstances should walkers leave the path, as there is a 300 feet drop nearly all the way round the headland, and it can be dangerous. For the really faint-hearted, there are four sturdily-built and strongly-railed observation platforms sited so that one can look right over the cliff edge at the sea-birds roosting on the ledges below. This was an impressive sight – with hundreds of guillimots and smaller numbers of razorbills packed in together and, as always, flying busily in and out. There are a small number of black guillimots which nest at St Bees (the only English colony) and a few nesting puffins, but in spite of diligent searching we could not find either of these.

126

In addition to the auks, birds to be seen around the cliffs at St Bees include rock pipits (above) kestrels, and occasional ravens.

About half-way round the cliff-walk, we were able to climb down to a small, rocky bay, and from the shore we watched the guillimots and razorbills on the surface of the sea. There was also a diver – probably a red-throated, although distance made identification difficult. The climb up from the bay tested our minimal rock-climbing abilities to the full, but there was considerable satisfaction in achievement!

Other birds that may be seen on or near the cliffs include kestrels, occasional ravens, rock pipits, corn buntings and linnets. A few years ago a pair of peregrines bred and successfully raised two chicks in a deserted raven's nest. There may also be sightings of Arctic and great skuas, sooty shearwaters, terns, gannets and Manx shearwaters.

After spending a fascinating afternoon on the cliffs, we eventually came to the lighthouse. By this time dusk was approaching, and rather than tackle the return journey around the fairly demanding pathway in failing light, we went inland and walked back to the car-park round the roads – a very long trek indeed!

Morecambe Bay RSPB Reserve

Managing body RSPB.
Access SD 4767. Best viewing near Hest Bank signal-box off A1505
Morecambe – Carnforth road.
Other information Best viewing at high spring tides.

Morecambe Bay is an astonishing place! When we arrived at the Hest Bank area of the RSPB reserve a few hours before high spring tide, all we could see was acre upon acre of bare sand-flats, beyond the salt marsh near the shore. Apart from a wide, shallow channel between Hest Bank and Morecambe, the sea seemed to have disappeared in the direction of Ireland. Although we could see some ducks in the channel, a few small parties of waders a long way out on the sand, some larger flocks flighting up and down the coast, and the occasional redshank probing around in the salt marsh, there was little to indicate that this was the widely-acknowledged finest site in Britain for seeing waders.

We had arrived early intentionally. Peak viewing time is a couple of hours before a high spring tide, when the waders are forced to come close in shore to roost as the sea covers up the vast feeding grounds of the intertidal area. Anyone planning to visit Morecambe would be wise to check the times and dates of the tides to avoid disappointment. Our early arrival was also partly prompted by descriptions we had heard about the behaviour of the incoming tide, and we were keen to see it. So, bearing in mind the warnings about quicksands, channels, and the speed with which the tide advances, we set off to walk out onto the sand-flats which provide such rich feeding grounds for the birds.

These flats are the largest part of the huge tidal plain stretching between Lancashire and Cumbria. The sand, which looks so lifeless, is in fact a teeming mass of small molluscs, worms and crustaceans below the surface. An ideal habitat for these invertebrates is provided by the mixture of silt and fresh water discharged by the Rivers Keer and Kent and the salt water of the bay itself. Some idea of the richness of the feeding may be judged from the estimated numbers of the mollusc, the Baltic tellin, found at certain times – an incredible 5,000 per square metre – together with huge quantities of laver spire shells, and the crustacean *Corophium volutator*.

We picked our way across the salt marsh with its pools and channels, and out onto the sand, where we could see the holes and sand spirals indicating the presence of the various marine worms. We walked across the seemingly endless flats, pausing every so

Whimbrels are often seen on passage at Morecambe Bay – one of the most exciting places in Britain for waders.

often to peer through our binoculars at the parties of waders in the distance – identifying dunlins and knots in the air, oystercatchers, curlews, godwits and shelducks on the sand. It was rather frustrating – we could see all those birds, but could not approach them more closely. In the channel we saw a few mallard and some goldeneyes. We also watched as people walked right out on the sands until they were tiny dots in the distance, giving some idea of the huge expanses. A local man told us that once the tide began to flow, it would come in more quickly than we could walk. By this time, we could see that the channel was beginning to fill up, so we headed back towards the banks.

Quite suddenly, we saw that the tide was coming in – and it certainly moved fast. With the tide, of course, came the birds. First noisy parties of oystercatchers arrived, coming in from the mussel beds at Heysham. They were joined by curlews and bar-tailed godwits, with a smaller number of grey plovers, and were soon followed by dense flocks of knots and dunlins, swooping and turning as they came in to land. Soon, every available area of dry salt marsh held its crowd of birds. As the tide advanced, they moved to yet higher ground. There, they were joined by ringed plovers and redshanks, and some turnstones that had been fossicking around near the strand line. Finally, as the tide reached its zenith and all the salt marsh was covered, great clouds of birds took off and moved further along the coast, settling on still-exposed rocks and sandbanks in the distance. Although perhaps, not quite as thrilling as it would have been in spring when the really massive numbers of knots come, it was nevertheless, a sight to remember.

A sight to remember, too, were the birdwatchers! A solid phalanx of them lined the vantage points on the bank – with telescopes and tripods, cameras and binoculars – all talking excitedly about what they could see, or thought they could see, and (one of the nicest features of the 'birding' fraternity as a whole) doing their best to point out their discoveries to the less eagle-eyed.

The full list of 160 or so species recorded at Morecambe gives little idea of the sheer spectacle of actually seeing the birds in such vast numbers. It is said that anything up to 200,000 waders may be present around the bay at peak times, with up to 15,000 birds at Hest Bank alone. Whimbrels are often seen on passage, and vast flocks of dunlins stop over on their way to Africa. In May of most years, according to the reserve leaflet, sanderlings pass through. From time to time, hunting merlins and peregrines put up the wader flocks in a whirling, panic-stricken and noisy flight to safety. Wildfowl are often present – wigeons, teal and mergansers are all seen, while divers are often sighted off shore.

Also part of the Morecambe Bay reserve, but more easily accessible from the Leighton Moss reserve, is a comparatively new area which is just being developed as a habitat. It consists of about 140 acres at Carnforth Marsh, just behind the sea-wall. Here, a man-made shallow pool with a number of small islands has been constructed, with the water level and salinity controlled by sluices. Almost immediately on completion, the number of birds recorded feeding and breeding rose, with such species as the spotted redshank, ruff, green sandpiper, garganey and spoonbill all seen, while lapwings, redshanks and oystercatchers are breeding in increased numbers. A hide has been erected with suitable screening, and in a few years' time, no doubt, this will be a major attraction.

Leighton Moss RSPB Reserve

Managing body   RSPB.
Access   SD 4875. Just off Yealand – Redmayne – Silverdale road, before station.
Other information   Visitor centre. Leaflet. Open all year, certain days only. RSPB members only before 11.00.

Through no fault of its own, Leighton Moss was something of a disappointment. We were there on a weekend during school holidays, and the considerable noise, particularly in the hides, ensured that many of the more shy and secretive birds were nowhere to be seen. Nevertheless, this is a reserve that really should not be missed, as it has so much to offer – not just birds, but plants, insects and mammals.

Leighton Moss is a flood-plain mere in the floor of a small wooded valley surrounded by limestone hills, except on the south-west seaward aspect where it is separated from Morecambe Bay by an embankment. It consists of three large meres and several smaller ones, ranging from about six inches to three feet in depth, reed-beds, fen, scrub and woodland. It provides excellent examples of natural succession from open water to mature woodland, and, at the seaward end, from salt marsh to fresh water.

Since Leighton Moss became an RSPB reserve in 1964, intensive management has been undertaken both to improve the habitats and to retain them. The scrape mere is partially artificial, having been formed by excavation – the removed earth being used to build up the retaining banks. Many of the islands in it are also of artificial origin, consisting of rock and soil that has been dumped in the shallow water. Others have been made by cutting clumps of iris from the mere side, floating them out into the water when the level is high, and staking them. The water levels of the various meres are controlled by sluices.

Current management consists mainly of preventing the encroachment of reed into the open water and the spread of willow scrub into the reed-beds. Spraying with selective herbicides is practised, and successive cutting of the stems under water. Willow scrub is felled and treated to prevent re-growth, but some, on the moss edge, is coppiced every five or six years to provide habitats for the birds and insects. Also in the moss edge area, many native trees and shrubs such as alder, silver birch, alder buckthorn and guelder rose are planted.

The reed-beds are very important, providing nesting sites and cover for the bitterns; the ten or eleven pairs nesting here are the only regular breeding pairs in northern England. We did not see any, but we did hear a male booming as we walked across the causeway which traverses the middle of the reserve, and on which there is a public hide. We watched and waited, hoping to see the bird from which this extraordinary sound was emanating, but we were unlucky, possibly because the booming has strange ventriloquial properties, and the bird is not necessarily just where the sound appears to come from. But it could just have been that the camouflage of the bird prevented us from seeing it standing, as it probably was, with its neck and beak vertical, blending beautifully with its surroundings.

Sadly, bitterns are now very rare, with a total of only about fifty pairs nationwide. They actually became extinct in Britain in 1850 because of the extensive marshland drainage in the Norfolk Broads, and were not heard again until the end of the century. They are still restricted to large tracts of reed-beds, the lack of which prevents their spread. They nest among the reeds, the female building large, untidy piles of sedges and rushes in which she lays four to six eggs. Bitterns have quite a varied diet – ranging from frogs and small fish, various water insects, beetles, water weeds and dragonflies to water voles and even small birds and nestlings.

The reed-beds also provide cover and nesting sites for the many water rails, for which the reserve is well known, and for reed warblers. Another Leighton Moss success story is with bearded tits, who also occupy the reed-beds. The first pair bred in 1973, and ten years later the breeding population has risen to nearly forty. The habitat also acts as roosts for a number of species – especially starlings and pied wagtails, which are joined during the autumn migration by swallows, sand martins and yellow wagtails. Such large numbers of small birds attract predators such as sparrow-hawks, barn owls, and the occasional merlin, peregrine or hobby.

The meres and their islands are important for both nesting and feeding. On our visit, the noise of people was matched only by that of the very large colony of black-headed gulls, which could be heard long before they were seen, perching on every available object, squabbling and displaying. Quieter nesting birds of these areas include coots, lapwings, snipe and moorhens, as well as ducks – mallard, teal, pochards, shovelers, tufteds, gadwalls and a few garganeys. One of the real rarities that has bred once or twice is the spotted crake. Waders are about in spring and autumn – the redshank, spotted redshank and greenshank being relatively common, with ruffs and wood and green sandpipers often seen.

Another attractive habitat is the willow scrub and fen edge, where the willow coppicing has encouraged grasshopper warblers, reed buntings, sedge warblers, redpolls, whitethroats and lesser whitethroats. The surrounding woodlands are full of birds, with more warblers, thrushes, flycatchers, tits, woodpeckers, jays and tawny owls. Occasional although fairly regular visitors to Leighton Moss include black terns, marsh harriers, single ospreys, and less commonly purple herons and spoonbills.

It is not only the bird-life that is rich and varied. Insects are a special feature of Leighton Moss, and are being studied intensively. The large tracts of open water encourage some beautiful dragonflies and damselflies, including the common sympetrum, four-spotted libellula and brown aeshna dragonflies, and the large red and common coenagrion, the common blue and common isnura damselflies. Among the butterflies, the most common is the

The woodlands at Leighton Moss are full of birds, including tawny owls (above), warblers, thrushes and flycatchers.

peacock, but others to be seen include the small tortoiseshell, orange tip, small copper, small pearl-bordered, brimstone and green-veined white. Over 300 species of moths have been recorded, with the local scarce prominent, fen wainscot and bulrush being of particular interest.

Of the mammals, red and roe deer are both seen, as are fallow occasionally, and there are five species of bat. Most exciting, perhaps, are the otters which feed on the eels; least welcome is the recent arrival of mink.

As might be expected, water plants are numerous – with species such as rigid horn-wort and amphibious bistort, while the fen edge is almost always colourful with a selection of valerian, marsh marigolds, yellow iris, mare's tail, purple loosestrife and water mint. There is a great show of orchids nearly every year, with southern marsh, spotted and a range of hybrids.

Beltingham

Managing body Northumberland Naturalists' Trust.
Access NY 7864. Turn south off A693, 3 miles west of Haydon Bridge to river bridge at Crow Hall, then to Beltingham via minor roads, through village into flood-plain, and park on roadside.

This small reserve appealed to us enormously. Its nine acres consist of a short stretch of river bank, mostly alder and birch scrub, and include several small, scrub-covered islands. When we were there on a warm, sunny day, the river level was very low indeed, but the little stretch of stream between the bank and the nearest island made a charming picture of a peaceful backwater. The banks on either side were overhung with green vegetation, interrupted by great vivid splashes of rosebay willow-herb and fine stands of mallow. The brilliant yellow clusters of red-spotted monkey flowers grew on the shingle spits of the rocky shallows in the little side-stream, and in the woods behind several willow warblers were singing.

The reserve is just one of several sites along the South Tyne and Allen rivers which show an unusual 'heavy-metal' flora such as mountain pansy, alpine penny-cress and spring sandwort. This is due to the influence of lead and zinc silt from the North Pennine lead mines.

As we walked along the riverside, often pushing our way through the dense growth of willow-herb, we caught a glimpse of a common sandpiper darting into the vegetation on the opposite

Common sandpiper: these dapper little birds are mostly migratory,
returning from Africa in the spring to nest along rivers and loch edges.

bank of the river. Several of these attractive birds came and went –
easily recognisable by their distinctive low flight with alternative
flicking of the wings and gliding. On landing, the conspicuous
extension of the white breast plumage up in front of the folded
wing and the typical bobbing action confirmed identification.

Common sandpipers are migratory and travel to Africa, although
recently a few have been recorded as staying in Britain for the
winter. They return here to nest along river or loch edges, mostly in
the uplands, although a small number nest lower down around
lakes and on estuaries. Courtship can be very spectacular, as the
males are often extremely aggressive, fighting among themselves,
both on the ground and in swift chases in the air. Their display
consists of circling higher and higher in the air – the movement
accompanied by a trilling song. The nest is chosen from a series of
scrapes made by both male and female, sometimes well hidden in
deep vegetation at a distance from the water. Both sexes incubate
the clutch of up to four eggs.

In addition to common sandpipers, birds one might expect to
see at Beltingham include goosanders, dippers, woodcocks and
oystercatchers.

Skipwith Common

Managing body   Yorkshire Trust for Nature Conservation.
Access   SE 6738 and SE 6437 (entrances). On A19 York – Riccall road turn left opposite Co-op into Station Road in Riccall. Reserve one mile on left. Trust sign.
Other Information   Leaflet available.

Skipwith Common, a large area of heath, marsh and woodland, is the site of an unusual nature trail, situated around the runways of an old airfield. Although not primarily a bird reserve, it has a good bird population, including nightjars, and is certainly worth a visit.

We approached it along King Rudding Lane from the village of Riccall, and parked near the first post of the nature trail. The smell from the meat works opposite was less than attractive, but visitors should not be put off, there is plenty of parking space further down the lane.

The nature trail is about two and a quarter miles long, and except during winter flooding, the hard paths are suitable for wheelchairs. There is a descriptive booklet, available from the Yorkshire Naturalists' Trust in York. The trail starts in an area of open heath with gorse, a few birch trees, grassland, and some clumps of rosebay willow-herb – most of the latter had 'gone over' at the time of our visit. A few linnets were flitting around and a dunnock popped in and out of the undergrowth – but we did not see any of the yellowhammers recorded in this area.

From the heathland we passed into a wood, mainly of birch, with some oaks, willows and hawthorn, and growing in the shaded parts we saw some Broad buckler fern. Near post three is a bracken-edged clearing, but this soon merged into more mixed woodland. Here we saw a number of small- and medium-sized birds – mostly blackbirds and thrushes, some delightful and extremely noisy wrens, several great and blue tits and willow warblers.

We crossed what had been the third runway of the airfield and immediately found ourselves in much denser woodland, of oak and birch. We were, I think, a little late in the year to see the broad-leaved helleborine and the twayblade which grows in this heavily shaded section of the reserve. We saw a number of passerines, and continued to do so all along the trail.

Every so often around the trail there was a little detour which left the main track and ran parallel or almost parallel with it for a short distance. The first of these took us off to the right and opened out into a more extensive area of heath, with a good cover of ling interspersed with small birches. Here we saw a number of tree

Yellowhammers are recorded at various points along the Skipwith
Nature Trail – and eventually we saw one!

pipits, whinchats, reed buntings and a yellowhammer.

In front of post seven were a few scarlet pimpernels, growing in
an area of grass stunted by rabbit grazing. Following the path to the
right, we noted a large patch of bushgrass bordering the heathland.
Woodcocks are often seen along this section, and away to the right
is a good place for nightjars. We noted the request in the guide for
anyone hearing these fascinating birds to leave them undisturbed;
attempts to approach them could easily lead to them deserting the
nearer song perches. There certainly was no sound of them as we
strolled along, but it was rather too early in the day. The un-birdlike
sound of the male has an uncanny way of quietly inserting itself
into one's consciousness, giving the impression that one has been
hearing it for some time without being fully aware of it.

Hearing a nightjar is one thing; seeing it quite another. The
cryptic coloration makes it extremely difficult to spot when on the
ground, and its habit of darting after moths at dusk – either from
the ground or from the branch of a tree where it crouches rather
than perches – makes seeing it in any detail far from easy. The

137

nightjar's short bill is unusual in opening both horizontally and vertically, giving it a huge gape, and the fringe of stiff bristles which border the mouth are another strange feature. To clean this fringe, the bird has yet another unusual modification – a deeply serrated underside to the middle claw of its foot.

The track opens out into heathland beyond the trees, and here the growth of the trees has been controlled, so that it will not be invaded by birch and thus make it into a habitat less suitable for nightjars. Grasshopper warblers may be heard in this section. Further away beyond the heathland is a nesting colony of black-headed gulls, and although the season was nearly at an end, they were still making their presence known with their raucous calls.

Along much of this trail there are reminders of the reserve's wartime role. On the left of the track there are remains of old bomb bays, which have been colonised by birch, and redpolls are often seen feeding on the seeds. A little further on, there is a small area of marshy ground dominated by cotton grass, where sedge warblers are occasionally seen.

Further along, a younger plantation, interspersed with heathland, allowed a good view of some small birds, including finches. Bullfinches are common and feed on the seeds of the heather and rushes. Alongside the path was a ditch, and beyond that a large acreage of marsh offers cover to mallard – a pair flew noisily off as we approached – and teal, while in autumn large numbers of wigeons arrive.

This part of the trail yields a variety of wetland plants, including the jointed and the soft rush, various species of sphagnum moss, marsh pennywort and spotted orchid. Solomon's seal can also be found. An interesting point is the presence of centaury in the cracks in the path, where the lime of the disintegrated concrete has reduced the acidity of the soil. Reed buntings are frequently seen around this area.

On both sides of the runway the country is wooded – young willow on the right, and mostly birch on the left. The former is growing in very wet conditions, and along here part of the concrete runway has been removed and a small pool excavated, with a small island in it. Various water plants have been introduced and it is hoped that, in time, the variety of marsh birds recorded will increase. Visitors are particularly requested not to go round the far side of the pool for this reason, as lack of disturbance is very important. The wet clay beside the runway is one of the few places on the reserve where signs may be seen of the small herd of roe deer – slot marks are often visible.

Another smaller runway runs off to the left; here much of the concrete has been removed, leaving a large area of gravel where there are seasonal pools. These had dried up when we were there, but at other times of the year they can provide the greatest concentration of birds – and the most easily seen if approached carefully – on the reserve. Curlews, redshanks and lapwings have been recorded in early summer, while gulls, moorhens, pied wagtails and partridges are seen feeding and bathing, martins and swifts feed on the insects, and green woodpeckers are sometimes seen searching for food along the edge of the runway. Just past this there is a grassy patch fringed by woodland, which is a good place for butterflies, and for willow warblers, whitethroats, yellow-hammers and linnets.

Scotland

St Abb's Head

Managing body   Scottish Wildlife Trust/National Trust for Scotland.
Access   NT 9169. Southern end of reserve near St Abbs village, from B6438.
Other information   Car-park. Leaflet.

I am not sure which reached us first as we approached the sea-bird colonies at St Abb's Head reserve – the noise of the thousands of birds, or the smell of decaying fish! I think it was the noise – marginally – but the intensity of both gave clear indication that we were in for a treat. St Abb's Head, owned by the National Trust and leased to the Scottish Wildlife Trust, is of national importance for cliff-nesting sea-birds, and it affords wonderfully close views of them. It also demands, in some places, a good head for heights.

As we emerged from the path onto the cliff edge, we looked almost straight across a small rock-edged bay to the towering cliff of White Heugh – and white it was, with a mixture of bird droppings and the white fronts of auks. The auks were coming and going from the cliff-face continuously, and a number were floating in rafts on the sea. It is estimated that there are nearly 3,000 of them there, mostly guillimots, clinging to every possible ledge. A lesser number of razorbills were also there, and on the rocks and rocky islands in the bay, in addition to gulls, there were a number of oystercatchers and a few eiders. On the rocky shores beneath the cliffs, redshanks, turnstones and purple sandpipers are frequently seen.

We went round to the other side of the White Heugh headland where, long before we saw it, we knew there must be a huge kittiwake colony. That wonderful sound of 'kitti-wa-ake' was unmistakable. They were sitting on nests precariously perched on the cliff-face, together with some herring gulls. The best viewing point for these lovely birds was near the edge of the cliff which dropped almost vertically a very long way down to the sea below – but the thrill of seeing such a wonderful colony was

The wonderful call of the kittiwake is unmistakable – *kitti-wa-ake* – exactly as the reference books describe it!

ample reward for the effort of overcoming vertigo!

The kittiwake is said to be the most common British gull, with approximately half a million nesting pairs. This is due to a remarkable increase in numbers during this century, following cessation of massive predation by shooting and egg collecting during the nineteenth century. It is distinctive in appearance, with a yellow bill, dark eyes, very short black legs, grey back, black wing tips and pure white underwing. The juvenile plumage is even more distinctive, showing a broad black band on the tail, and a black leading edge to the wing. Apart from nesting, it spends hardly any time on land, a way of life reflected by exceptionally short legs and the absence of a hind toe.

From this headland the reserve opened out, allowing a choice of keeping fairly close to the cliff edge, or walking inland a little through more grassy country, where wheatears and pipits may be seen. We chose to keep near to the cliffs, and from the headland, some little paths dropped steeply down to delightful little rocky bays and inlets, where we saw more eiders. At other places, we found convenient vantage points overlooking the sea, where we sat and admired the superb view, and watched the bird traffic that was flying past. At one such point, we spotted a pair of puffins paddling quietly out of view around a rocky promontory. We waited a short time, and they came back into view. As there are only a few pairs at St Abb's Head (most of which nest near the lighthouse) we counted ourselves lucky to have seen them. In addition to nesting birds, an exciting variety pass by off shore, including sooty and Manx shearwaters, Arctic and great skuas and gannets. Migration times can be especially rewarding, with such rarities as red-breasted flycatchers and yellow-browed warblers recorded, and thousands of more common species use the area as a resting point on their east coast migration flight. Wherever we had a really good view of the rocky shores below, we searched carefully with binoculars for purple sandpipers, but we did not see any.

Approaching the lighthouse, we came to yet another gigantic cliff-face with a mixed population of nesting birds – kittiwakes, razorbills, guillimots, shags and herring gulls, each occupying its own niche in this 'high-rise' accommodation.

After several hours spent both on the cliffs and in watching some of the smaller birds such as stonechats, pipits and wheatears away from the cliffs, we climbed up past the lighthouse, following the road until we saw the long, narrow stretch of water that is Loch More. As we approached, we heard a cacophony of kittiwake calls, and soon saw it was coming from a vast flock of the birds splashing vigorously about in the centre of the loch. There was a constant traffic of the birds coming and going – having a thorough bathe before returning to the cliffs and their nests. Every so often, something would alarm them and the whole flock would take to the air before returning to settle again further along. It was a remarkable sight. Their presence has had an interesting effect on the ecology of the loch – their droppings have so enriched the water that there is a profuse growth of microscopic algae which filters out the light, thus preventing the growth of all but a few species of waterweed.

Although the birds are the great attraction at St Abbs, there are plenty of other features of interest. The area of sea around St Abb's Head itself is part of the reserve, with deep, clear waters which are rich in marine plants and animals offering marvellous opportunities for underwater studies. There is a great variety of land plants in the different habitats, which result from the widely varying rocks and soils. In the poorer more acid areas of grassland, tormentil, heather, and heath bedstraw are among the plants to be seen, while in the richer parts, there is lady's bedstraw, rock rose and spring sandwort. The cliff-faces and edges have a colourful maritime flora of thrift, sea carrot and, in places, Scots lovage.

Loch Leven and Vane Farm

Managing body   NCC/RSPB.
Access   NT 1699 (Vane Farm RSPB). Leave M90 at Junction 5. Access to
Vane Farm car-park on south side of B9097 Glenrothes road. NO 1501
(NCC). Access to nature reserve restricted to Kirkgate Park, Burleigh Sands
and Loch Leven Castle.
Other information   Vane Farm open January – March, weekends; April –
December, daily (except Friday). Observation room. Shop. Hide by
lochside for members.

Mention Scotland and grey geese, and one reserve in particular
springs to mind – Loch Leven on Tayside. Every winter up to
13,000 pink-footed and a regular 2,000 or so greylag geese arrive
from their breeding grounds in Greenland and Iceland to feed on
the loch and the surrounding agricultural land. The arrival and
movements of skein after skein of these lovely birds provides one
of the really great spectacles of bird-life in Britain.

Geese are by no means all that this exciting reserve has to offer. It
is unusual in being of international importance for both breeding
and wintering wildfowl, with more than ten species of duck being
recorded, in addition to the geese. There is a small breeding colony
of terns, a huge breeding colony of black-headed gulls on one of
the islands, large numbers of great crested grebes, a variety of
passerines, and an interesting assortment of waders. The loch is
also world famous for its trout fishing and is of considerable
botanical interest.

The wildlife of Loch Leven is managed by two bodies. It is a
National Nature Reserve, controlled by the Nature Conservancy
Council, and, at its southern end, there is the RSPB reserve and
education centre at Vane Farm, opened in 1967. This centre is the
first of its kind in Britain, employing a full-time teacher to conduct a
programme of visits and talks for schools.

The Loch is of unusual interest in demonstrating how birds can,
over the centuries, adapt themselves to changing conditions, and
how an impressive number of different species can co-exist in a
relatively small area by exploiting different foodstuffs. Sadly but
inevitably, it also illustrates the pressures put on the environment
by industry and farming. This is all described in a useful booklet
Wildlife of Loch Leven, published by the RSPB and available at the Vane
Farm centre.

The account of the wildfowl points out that, with its area of over
3,500 acres of water, burns, marsh, moss and agricultural land, Loch
Leven offers the wildfowl their three basic requirements. These are

– water, a variety of sheltered habitats both on the water, on the islands and among the fringe vegetation, and, of supreme importance, a good and varied supply of food.

When the geese arrive at Loch Leven in late September and early October, they are exhausted, dehydrated, and in very poor condition after their long flight across the Atlantic. They rest on St Serf's, the largest of the islands in the Loch, for a couple of days, before dispersing to the stubble fields in Kinrosshire, where they feed extremely well on the grain that has been left after the barley and oat harvest. This may last them right through to February, depending on how quickly the farmers do their winter ploughing.

At the same time, the farmers in the area are busy providing the geese with their next source of food – the remains of the potato harvest. Potatoes that are too small or have been broken and left to rot, suit the geese very well indeed. Later in the winter, even more potatoes become available, as they are thrown up when the farmers plough the fields for the next crop. Thus far, the geese are not causing the local farmers any trouble; in fact, they may actually be helping them by removing discarded grain and potatoes which could carry disease forward into the following year's crop.

However, with the arrival of the first bite of spring grass, farmers and geese come into competition. But the first and most tempting growth only takes place over about a fortnight – and after that, there is sufficient for all. Finally, before they set off for their breeding grounds, the geese may also feed on the newly sown seed for the year's crops – this too is not viewed with any pleasure by farmers. If the seed is treated with toxic chemicals, it does not do the geese much good either.

So, the present day geese have an adequate supply of food throughout their stay, and it is interesting to note that, as the face of agriculture has changed, so have their feeding habits. In the days before the present field system of agriculture, the birds were able to find enough food in the acres of marshland near the loch.

Other wildfowl, such as the dabbling ducks, while feeding on the same food sources as the geese, feed principally at night and roost on the loch during the day, thus avoiding direct competition. The diving ducks, such as the pochard and goldeneye, feed in the deeper water of the loch, while the swans (mute and wintering whooper) feed in the shallower areas.

Although feeding for the wildfowl is still adequate, some concern is felt for the future, because of what is happening to the loch itself. It is the centre of the area, and into it drains quite a range of pollutants – sewage, drainage water from surrounding agricultural land which frequently contains high concentrations of chemicals, and so on. The effect of this has been to change the

Up to 2,000 greylags arrive at Loch Leven every autumn from their breeding grounds in Greenland and Iceland.

chemical balance of the water to a much higher level of nutrients, which encourages the growth of algae in particular – clearly visible under certain conditions as a bloom on the water surface. This, in turn, prevents light reaching some of the water plants, with the result that once common plants, such as Canadian pondweed and stonewort, are now virtually non-existent. There has been a drop in the number of wildfowl which fed on them; in addition, invertebrates such as mayflies and dragonflies have disappeared, and the quality of the famous fish has also declined. As the booklet says 'After all, you cannot treat the loch as a sewer and still expect to take so many fish from it'.

The breeding duck on Loch Leven include about 30 pairs of gadwalls, which represent an estimated 60 per cent of the Scottish population, and about 500 pairs of 'tufties', 20 per cent of the British breeding population. Other species include up to 450 pairs of mallard, 40 pairs of wigeons, 12 pairs of shovelers, and a few pairs of teal. Moorhens and coots also breed, as do 20 pairs of great crested grebes. The ducks crowd onto St Serf's Island to breed, and

145

when the ducklings hatch, there is plenty of shelter in the shape of overhanging vegetation on the water's edge where they can hide from predators.

Apart from the two principal species of grey geese, others such as white fronts and barnacles are relatively common, while brents and snow geese are occasionally recorded. The loch edges and the remaining wetland areas provide habitats for a number of waders, such as snipe, curlews, redshanks, ruffs, dunlins, greenshanks and golden plovers, while there are records of green sandpipers, black-tailed godwits and spotted redshanks.

We visited the loch in early spring, when there were still a number of geese, and their flighting in and out gave us some idea of what it must be like when they arrrive in the autumn. As night fell, we walked along to the point nearest to Castle Island, and in the darkness the sound of the birds was magical – the subdued honking of the geese, the calls of the various waders and, quite close in shore, the extraordinary 'growling' of the great crested grebes.

The limited public access to the loch shore – necessary to avoid undue pressure on the birds, who use the secluded bays for roosting and shelter, is, none the less, a little disappointing. It must, however, be accepted as being in the best interests of the wildlife.

However, the RSPB centre at Vane Farm gives excellent views of the loch from a high viewpoint and, for Society members, there is an excellent hide, reached by an underpass under the main road. From the centre building (an old sheep steading) with its displays, there are good views out towards St Serf's Island particularly, where we could see many geese and the black-headed gulls.

We followed the nature trail at Vane Farm which took us almost to the summit of the 824 foot hill behind the centre, with magnificent views of the surrounding countryside. Birds were plentiful in the gorse, rough moorland and birch wood – including tits, wrens, robins, willow warblers, pied wagtails and one or two yellowhammers. Returning from the trail, we crossed to the hide overlooking a man-made lagoon and scrape where a number of water birds congregate, including some of the passage waders. We saw tufted ducks, shelducks and redshanks.

So important is Loch Leven for wildfowl that relatively little notice has been taken of its plant-life. This is varied, including a good range of water plants such as marsh thistle and waterlily, and a number of rarities such as holygrass, slender rush and mudwort. On the hill behind the RSPB centre, a range of typical heathland plants – lady's and heath bedstraw, tormentil and bracken – is found. The majority of species are described in some detail in *Wildlife of Loch Leven*.

Falls of Clyde

Managing body   Scottish Wildlife Trust.
Access   NS 8842. Leave Lanark on A73 and after ¼ mile turn right onto minor road to New Lanark.
Other information   Visitor centre. Leaflet. Video film.

We were lucky to visit this reserve when the river was in full spate, with the water thundering down through the wooded gorge and over the three magnificent waterfalls in its full imposing glory. For much of the summer, the level of the river is low, with the bulk of the water being diverted for hydro-electric purposes just above the topmost fall and returned downstream of the lowest. But our visit coincided with one of the several times during the year when the water is released by the electricity authorities, and the Falls of Clyde can be seen in all their magnificence.

We spent some time in the Scottish Wildlife Trust's visitor centre, looking at the exhibits, watching a very interesting video of the wildlife of the area, and searching the rocky outcrops adjacent to the lowest of the three falls – Dundaff Linn – for signs of the many

Winter visitors at the Falls of Clyde include bramblings.

dippers which frequent the river. Binoculars are provided for visitors to inspect the river through the centre's windows. We were in luck, and soon spotted one of these charming little birds, bobbing up and down and occasionally disappearing under the surface.

There is a path open to the public along the north-east bank of the river, offering wonderful views of it, often from right above the falls. It winds through mixed woodland for the most part, and there are plenty of woodland birds, but with the river in full spate their songs could not be heard, so a quick eye was necessary to catch sight of them. Soon after we left the visitor centre, we saw a couple of grey wagtails – one on some rocky ledges on the opposite bank, flicking its tail as it hopped about, and showing the distinctive yellow under-tail coverts and the black bib of the male's summer plumage. The birds find the bulk of their food near water – gnats, small crustaceans, molluscs, water beetles and mayflies. In contrast to the other wagtails, they frequently perch in trees and dart out to catch small insects. Nesting is usually in cavities in the banks or holes in stone walls, and sometimes in the deserted nest of a dipper. If they build their own nest, it is of moss and lined with hair. Two broods are common, with a third not unknown.

We climbed quite steeply up the side of the gorge through mixed broad-leaved and conifer woodland, and looked down on the boiling river – noting some of the inaccessible ledges which, later in the year, could afford nesting sites for kestrels. Later on too, some interesting plants would grow on them – purple saxifrage and butterwort. We saw some tits – including long-taileds, a great spotted woodpecker, a number of goldcrests, and kept a close look-out for the very local willow tit. We were probably a bit early in the year for the garden warblers, chiffchaffs and spotted flycatchers. Coal tits, siskins, redpolls, stock doves and kingfishers are present throughout the year, while winter visitors include fieldfares, redwings and bramblings.

The path took us about a mile and a half up the side of the gorge, past the double steps over Cora Linn fall and right up to the top one, at Bonnington Linn. Beyond this the river becomes much quieter, with little sandy beaches and overhung banks where otters may be seen. Badgers, roe deer and red squirrels are also present on the reserve, as well as pipistrelle and Natterer's bats.

The Falls of Clyde reserve is botanically rich, with the damp environment suiting ferns, mosses, lichens and liverworts. Typical woodland flowers are present – celandine, bluebell, wood avens and, in the damper parts, marsh marigold, while in the more acid areas, typical plants such as bilberry and heather grow in profusion.

Mull of Galloway RSPB Reserve

Managing body   RSPB.
Access   NX 1630. South of Stranraer, via A716 to Drummore, then B7041
to lighthouse.
Other information   The cliffs are dangerous.

The RSPB reserve at Mull of Galloway, on the most south-westerly
tip of Scotland south of Stranraer, consists of forty acres and is an
SSSI, listed in the Nature Conservancy Council's Review as a site of
national importance.

Our visit here brought home to us once more that birdwatchers
should always hope for the best, even in the most unpromising
conditions. We arrived at the reserve in winds so strong that the
vehicle seemed to be in real danger of blowing over, and fog so
thick that we could see about twenty yards at the most. However,
we decided to wait, hoping that the fog might be blown away.

Our patience was rewarded, Suddenly the grey curtain lifted, the
sun shone through, and there in front of us, not more than 100
yards away, was the Mull of Galloway Lighthouse and its
surrounding buildings. We also had a good view of the headland
with its 200 foot granite cliffs, which support small colonies of sea-
birds – small because the cliff-faces offer few ledges suitable for
nesting sites.

We walked down the tussocky slopes and found a sheltered
hollow near the edge, where we could watch the birds flighting in
and out from the cliff-face. Black-backed and herring gulls glided
past almost within touching distance, as did a few fulmars and

Herring gulls glided past almost within touching distance
near the cliff edge.

kittiwakes. Most of the activity, however, was down near the sea, where guillemots and razorbills, especially the former, were rushing in and out, apparently from nests that we could not see.

The sea's surface was studded with rafts of birds, and to our great delight we spotted one of the reserve's specialities – a black guillemot – its black summer plumage with white wing patches making it easily identifiable. Smaller by some three inches than the more common guillemot, the scarlet-footed black guillemot is unique among British auks in at least two ways. Firstly, it shows an almost total reversal of plumage in the winter, the back being barred black and white, while the head and underparts are white; the white wing patches remain on the black wings. Secondly, it is the only British auk that lays two eggs (the others lay just one) and it usually manages to rear both chicks. Very much a bird of the more northern coasts and off-shore islands, the black guillemot lays its blotched buff or blue-green eggs in caves and crevices or occasionally in shallow burrows. Nesting is preceded by a variety of displays, often involving a number of pairs.

Only a few pairs of black guillemots nest at Mull of Galloway, nor is it one of the biggest nesting sites for the razorbills, kittiwakes, shags and cormorants, but it is a very enjoyable place to visit, and there is the added attraction of the possibility of seeing gannets and Manx shearwaters on migration at the appropriate times.

In addition, the cliff-tops are of special interest to the botanist. There are significant colonies of spring squill, purple milk vetch, golden samphire, rock samphire and rock spurry – each at the northern limit of their British range – while Scots lovage and rose are at the southern boundary of their range.

Caerlaverock National Nature Reserve and Wildfowl Trust Refuge

---

Managing body   Wildfowl Trust/NCC.
Access   NY 0566 (Wildfowl Trust). From B725 at Bankend. NY 0464 (NCC). From B725 and Caerlaverock Castle.
Other information   Wildfowl Trust: escorted tours September – April daily (except 24 and 25 December). Hides. Observatory. NCC: free access except sanctuary area. Salt marsh can be dangerous.

Caerlaverock National Nature Reserve spread over 12,000 acres of tidal marshland and sandbank, and 1,500 acres of salt marsh on the Solway Firth, also has within its boundaries the 800 acres Wildfowl Trust Reserve. The Wildfowl Trust has a further 235 acres of farmland south of the River Lochar and 460 acres of farmland and salt marsh (merse) north of the river.

The whole area is internationally famous as the wintering ground for the entire population of approximately 8,000 barnacle geese from Spitzbergen, and for the presence (at its northern breeding limit) of the natterjack toad. It also accommodates large numbers of wintering greylag and pink-footed geese (up to 5,000 of the latter) as well as hundreds of whooper and Bewick's swans, other wildfowl, waders such as golden plovers, curlews and lapwings, and an exciting variety of raptors.

The story of the development of Caerlaverock as a Wildfowl Trust Reserve is told by Colin Campbell, the warden-manager, in the the Wildfowl Trust's magazine *Wildfowl World* of Winter 1984. The area was designated a National Nature Reserve in 1957, and the Wildfowl Trust Reserve at Eastpark Farm was established in 1971, when the late Duke of Norfolk offered the tenancy to the Trust.

The first task was to build two screening banks (similar to those introduced by Sir Peter Scott at Slimbridge) along the farm roads, so that visitors could not be seen by the feeding barnacle geese. Into these banks (which were grassed over) were placed a series of fibreglass hides. The first two banks screened the road from the farm to the two-storied observation tower, already erected on the NNR by the Nature Conservancy Council and giving splendid views over the merse. The ponds created by the building of the banks would attract wildfowl in due course, and to establish and encourage invertebrate life in them a number of islands of farmyard manure were constructed. In a successful effort to attract more wild birds, some tame decoys were introduced and, when their task was completed, they were removed to other centres, so that Caerlaverock now has genuinely wild birds only.

As soon as the centre was in operation, important research programmes started, and a great deal of information has been gathered in the succeeding years, not just about barnacle geese, but about other wildfowl as well. A ringing programme was instigated, with a visit to the breeding grounds at Spitzbergen, and this has produced vital facts about the population of this beautiful goose.

So successful has the centre been that the number of birds wintering has increased dramatically, and it has attracted both Bewick's and whooper swans. A trap was constructed for the whoopers in 1979, and now they are also being studied. The numbers of ducks have risen to a recorded 1,400 pintails, 1,000 wigeons and 1,300 teal.

The salt marsh attracts huge numbers of waders – curlews, oystercatchers, redshanks and knots, while the raptors seen include kestrels, peregrines, hen harriers, the occasional merlin

A trap for whooper swans was constructed in 1979, and they are being studied in detail at Caerlaverock.

and short-eared owls. Rarities include the blue-winged teal, spoonbill, buff-breasted sandpiper, long-billed dowitcher and little bunting.

We visited the Trust's reserve towards the end of the winter, when an appreciable number of the barnacles had already left on their long flight back to Spitzbergen. Even so, there were still many hundreds of birds there, and it was sheer joy to watch and to listen to them from the tower as they grazed in the fields.

We spent a great deal of time in the various small hides, and from one were lucky enough to see barnacle, pink-footed and greylag geese grazing together, which enabled us to see clearly the differences between the latter two. Apart from the difference in size, with the pink-footed being considerably smaller, the greylag has a pink-orange bill, while the pink-footed's is pink and black. In flight, the greylag forewing is noticeably paler than the other grey geese, while the rump and back are also paler. The head and bill of the greylag are markedly heavier than those of the pink-footed.

As we walked down between the two high banks towards the observation tower, we saw and heard several willow warblers in the bushes, several robins and a goldcrest. From the tower, we looked out across the wild merse to the goose sanctuary, where many more hundreds of barnacles, and lesser numbers of pink-foots and greylags were grazing. Later, we drove round to the part of the NNR where there is public access and ventured, with great care, out onto the mud-flats. Great care is needed, and it is not advisable to go out without first contacting the warden. We went when the tide was falling, but the weather was terrible – pouring with rain and blowing a gale, so we saw nothing at all. We hope to go back one day in the summer, and hear the natterjack toads.

Glen Muick and Lochnagar

Managing body   Scottish Wildlife Trust.
Access   NO 3185. Glen Muick road from Ballater (single track). Parking at public car-park at Spittal of Glen Muick and not on roadside.
Other information   Leaflet. Care necessary because of rapidly changing weather conditions.

Some of the Highland nature reserves are enormous, and one could spend years wandering through them and still not see all they have to offer. The 6,250 acre Glen Muick and Lochnagar reserve near Ballater is such a one. It is part of the Balmoral Estates, and is managed by the Scottish Wildlife Trust. It is in an area of breath-taking beauty, dominated by the 2,789 foot Cac Carn Beag at the summit of the Lochnagar massif, and by the very deep Loch Muick. From almost any point there are spectacular views of mountains and glens, and the entire reserve has a wealth of wildlife in its varied habitats. There are many birds within its boundaries, but it is equally renowned for its range of geological features, its outstanding plants and its animals. Consequently, it would give a very false picture to concentrate just on the birds in this all-embracing tract of the Highlands.

On the warm and sunny summer's day we visited Loch Muick, the reserve looked magnificent, and we felt we could not wait to begin exploring it. But, a word of warning – which is emphasised in both the visitor centre and in the reserve handbook – some of the paths which take walkers up into the mountains are very testing, and anyone venturing on the high level walks, even if they set off in good weather, should be adequately equipped with maps, compasses and proper hill-climbing clothing, as bad weather and disorientating mists can descend with frightening rapidity. As we were not so equipped, we decided to keep to the lower walks, and although by so doing we missed some of the rare birds, animals and plants of the higher hills, I shall mention many things which can be seen on the reserve rather than just those we actually saw on our visit.

The birds can be divided into four groups – those to be found in the woodlands, the moors, the water, and the more mountainous areas. Although there is little woodland on the reserve, some of it surrounds the visitor centre, and depending on the time of year, redpolls, siskins and dozens of chaffinches are present. Crossbills may be seen by the quick-of-eye but are more frequently heard, while spotted flycatchers are by no means uncommon, both around the centre and in the small conifer wood on the southern shore of Loch Muick.

A walk through some of the remoter woodlands in the reserve may provide the lucky visitor with that most surprising of British avian sights – that of a large turkey-sized bird becoming noisily airborne and winging its way through the pine trees with remarkable agility for one so large. It is a capercaillie – a notoriously elusive bird in spite of its size. They may sometimes be seen feeding among heather and in woodland clearings with an understorey of bilberry and crowberry.

These remarkable birds, which together with the ptarmigan and the golden eagle are so evocative of the Highlands, became extinct in Scotland at the end of the eighteenth century, due in part to the clearance of their principal habitat, the pine forests, and in part to hunting. Fortunately, in 1837, a number were reintroduced from Sweden to the Marquis of Breadalbane's estate in Perthshire. The species quickly made itself at home once more, and today there are an appreciable number in the west and central Highlands, and a few have even spread to the Lowlands.

The male capercaillie, which, at thirty-three inches is about eight inches larger than the female, is easily recognisable with its dark grey-black plumage, shimmering blue-green breast and grey-white bill surrounded by scarlet skin. The female's cryptic plumage is much drabber – mottled buff colouring above and lighter mottling below, and a distinctive rufous pattern on the chest. Although extremely noisy when taking off from the trees – in which they often perch among the highest boughs – their flight is silent, and shows the typical gamebird flapping followed by an angled glide.

Spotted flycatchers are not uncommon at Glen Muick around the visitor centre and in the small conifer wood on the loch's southern shore.

The territorial displays of the male capercaillie are one of the more bizarre sights and sounds of British bird-life. Singly or in groups, they parade in forest clearings, their bristling throat feathers, puffed up plumage and fanned tail making them appear even larger than they are. Their aggressive appearance is no bluff – they will threaten intruders of almost any size. Aggressive displays towards other males include leaping into the air, fanning their tails and uttering a series of extraordinary cries which have been described variously as a series of clops, pops, wheezes, a rattle followed by a sound like the drawing of a cork, and ending with the sound of a knife being ground – it needs to be heard to be appreciated in full.

Black grouse are closely related to the capercaillie and they too may be seen at the woodland edges and, for the early riser, along the lochside. The red grouse is common on the reserve, but it is very much a bird of the moorland where it feeds on heather shoots. The most plentiful of the moorland birds, however, is the meadow pipit, while during the summer months migrant wheatears are very much in evidence. Another migrant, but less commonly seen, is the ring ouzel, which frequents the rocky streams, near to which it nests soon after its arrival in May.

The most spectacular of the moorland birds which may be seen on the reserve is the magnificent golden eagle. Few are lucky enough to see one at really close quarters; they are most likely to be seen soaring over the hills in the distance. As we were driving back along the single-track road from the reserve we caught several glimpses of a really big bird, appearing and disappearing over the hills far away to our right. It was too far away to claim with any degree of confidence, but its movements were typical, and it certainly seemed too large for a buzzard.

Other birds of prey inhabiting the area include peregrines, merlins and hen harriers – the latter two most likely to be seen in late summer en route to the south from their breeding grounds.

For those who venture into the more mountainous regions of the reserve the rewards are considerable, but some of the higher nesting species are occasionally seen at lower levels. One of the birds which manages to survive the harshest conditions is the ptarmigan, which nests from about 2,500 feet upwards, and is often seen in its summer plumage of brownish-black, with white wings and underparts. The red grouse also nests at high level, up to about 3,000 feet, and dunlins too, although they prefer nest sites near lochans or in marshes. Golden plovers are another high nesting species, but non-breeding parties are seen at lower levels during the early summer. Dotterels and snow buntings have been recorded as nesting species on some of the highest reaches of Lochnagar in years gone by.

Loch Muick is a considerable expanse of water and one might expect to see many water birds in and around it; but its altitude, and the fact that it has few shallow areas make it largely unattractive save for a few mallard and teal, and of rather more interest, some goosanders. The other wet areas of the reserve, such as the streams and bogs, attract common sandpipers, lapwings, oystercatchers and redshanks, while dippers frequent the rocky streams.

The mammalian population is dominated, as might be expected, by the handsome red deer, many of which can usually be seen throughout the reserve. Other mammals include those most charming of creatures, red squirrels, still to be found in the conifers in this area, and mountain hares, conspicuous in their white winter coats as late as the beginning of May. The fox, so common further south, is only present in small numbers, while a sighting of an otter or a wild cat – both present – would be a bonus indeed.

Anyone familiar with the Highlands is also, to their cost, familiar with the most numerous of the insects, the viciously biting midges, (Clucoides spp.) but Glen Muick and Lochnagar have a surprising range of other invertebrate life. This includes the northern eggar, emperor and fox moths, dragon- and damselflies, and the rare whirligig beetle, *Gyrinus opacus*, which is present in considerable numbers.

The reserve is rightly famous for its plant life, with over 200 vascular species recorded, in a variety of habitats, although Loch Muick itself is poor, with stoneworts being the most interesting of its few species. The remainder of the reserve more than makes up for it, however, with, at the higher levels, bearberry and mountain azalea, and above the 3,000 foot mark least willow, stiff sedge and hair moss. Lichens such as cladonias and cetrairias thrive, while ferns such as alpine lady and parsley ferns are among those found. Some rarities grow on the cliffs, out of reach of predation by the deer. There are also the saxifrages, alpine lady's mantle, butterwort and the clubmoss *Lycopodium*.

The handbook of the reserve, available at the visitor centre, describes several walks. We chose two – the short but quite steep one up to the Capel Mount viewpoint about half an hour distant from the centre, from where we had wonderful views of the various mountain peaks; on returning from there, we tackled the complete circuit of Loch Muick, a distance of about eight miles, and worth every step. The pathways are good for the most part, and although we did not see many birds, we enjoyed the scenery, with its spectacular waterfalls, streams, mountain tops, and, of course, the Loch itself.

Fowlsheugh RSPB Reserve

Managing body   RSPB.
Access   NO 8880. Signposted from A92 about 3 miles south of Stonehaven.
Other information   The cliffs are dangerous.

For the lover of sea-birds and coastal scenery, this reserve near Stonehaven in Grampian is essential viewing. It has been described as a 'sea-bird city', and achieved national, indeed international, fame when the BBC's *Birdwatch* programme was transmitted from the cliffs in 1982.

The reserve itself consists of a narrow grassy strip, in places only a few yards wide and about a mile and a half long, from which the birds on the 200 foot high cliffs can be seen – often at very close quarters. As with all cliff-top viewing, great care needs to be taken to keep away from crumbling edges.

The cliff-faces are absolutely crammed with birds during the breeding season, and it is estimated that there are about 30,000 pairs each of guillemots and kittiwakes, 5,000 pairs of razorbills, about 400 or so pairs of herring gulls, nearly 300 pairs of fulmars, some shags, as well as many non-breeding birds. Much of the cliff-face is not suitable for puffins, as it offers little in the way of burrowing sites, but nevertheless about 150 pairs have been recorded as breeding there, and we certainly saw a few. The sea below is a mass of birds, and the inwards and outwards traffic is non-stop.

It is a wonderful reserve and a marvellous place to see.

Loch Garten RSPB Reserve

Managing body   RSPB.
Access   NH 9818. Signposted off Boat of Garten – Nethy Bridge road.
Other information   Observation hide open daily, mid-April – late August, if ospreys nest. Access within sanctuary strictly on marked path. Leaflets. Shop.

Loch Garten to British birdwatchers means just one thing – ospreys! The story of how, in the 1950s, a band of dedicated people nurtured the re-establishment of the osprey as a breeding species in Scotland is told by Philip Brown and George Waterston – the principal architects of the successful operation – in The Return of the Ospreys and by Philip Brown in The Scottish Osprey.

Ospreys were exterminated in Scotland by the end of the last century following a combination of persecution by gamekeepers, sportsmen and egg and skin collectors. It was not until the early 1950s that any sign of a possible return was mooted, when a few single summering birds were seen around Speyside. Then, in 1954, a pair nested and reared young. Thoughts of conservation were uppermost among the few people who knew of this and in 1957 'Operation Osprey', organised under the auspices of the RSPB with help from other conservation bodies, began in earnest.

Following abortive attempts at other sites in previous years, a male osprey gave some indication of preparing a nest in a pine tree south of Loch Garten. The watchers believed, through past experience, that this was the normal preliminary to the female arriving. Immediately, George Waterston, who was in charge of field operations, established a camp site nearby and enlisted a team of trusted ornithologists to keep a 24-hour watch on the nest throughout the season. The watchers' main concern was to guard against disturbance of the birds by genuine birdwatchers, but, much more vitally, against the deliberate and well-planned raids which were expected by egg collectors, who cared nothing for the birds, but a great deal for the money that such prizes would bring. In 1957, however, the watchers were doomed to disappointment. The single osprey, after showing interest, disappeared in the middle of May.

The following year, however, was a different story: a pair did nest, in the same stunted pine tree. Assuming that the first egg had been laid on 10 May, the watchers calculated that the first chick would hatch on 14 June after thirty-five days. It was in the early hours of 3 June that Philip Brown, peering through the lightening gloom, suddenly saw the female osprey take off from the nest, screaming with alarm. Almost simultaneously, he saw the lower branches of the tree shaking violently. Frantically pulling the communication cord attached to the wrist of his companion sleeping in a nearby tent, he tore off at top speed across the intervening marsh to apprehend what was clearly a nest robber. But the boggy ground held him and his companion back, and they were still thirty yards away when they saw the robber drop out of the tree and disappear into the surrounding forest – pursuit was unsuccessful.

As daylight dawned, a whitish patch on the ground below the tree proved to be the smashed remains of an egg with a well-developed embryo. The despair of this find was alleviated slightly by a quick check on the nest – made while the parent birds were off – which revealed that two eggs still remained, so at least it was not a total disaster – or so it seemed. Within twenty-four hours it was clear that the sitting birds were not happy; they were restless and constantly fidgeting. After watching this for some time, George Waterston and Bert Axell waited until both birds were away from the nest, and went out to investigate. The cause of the birds' distress was soon apparent; they returned with what appeared to be the two remaining osprey eggs, but which, in closer inspection in full daylight, proved to be two hen eggs, daubed with brown shoe polish. As Philip Brown said, 'It was the end, and we tasted in full the bitterness of utter defeat'.

The following year even more elaborate plans were made for protecting the eyrie, and to a lesser extent, a 'frustration eyrie' the robbed pair built in the pine trees to the east of the Loch. Eyries of this kind are a feature of osprey behaviour and are often built, but not used, by birds whose principal breeding attempt has been thwarted. The birds finally settled for the 'frustration' eyrie, thus provoking a monumental reorganisation of protective measures. But, patience and skill were finally rewarded, and the ospreys successfully hatched and reared three chicks, in the eyrie that has been occupied almost continuously since. About fifty young have been reared, providing the basis for the recolonisation of the Highlands by this magnificent bird.

I make no apology for including this brief outline of the return of the osprey, an important chapter in British ornithology. Without the tenacity of that dedicated band of people, the Loch Garten reserve would not exist. The modern visitor centre and the George Waterston Hide from which the ospreys may now be viewed are famous throughout the country. It is a far cry from the long night-watches and the binder-twine alarm system of the early years. Now the eyrie is guarded by electronic devices, which also enable visitors in the hide to hear the sound of the nesting birds and the chicks while viewing them from a distance. We were fortunate enough to see not just the two adults, the male sitting on his favourite perch a short distance from the eyrie – but the season's two chicks, which were well-grown and already taking short flights.

Exciting though the ospreys are, they are by no means the only wildlife to be seen at Loch Garten, and a visit is rewarding at almost any time of the year. The loch is situated in Abernethy Forest, one of the rare remnants of the ancient Caledonian pine and birch forests which covered vast areas of Scotland 8,000 years ago. The reserve has, within 1,500 acres, five main habitats – Scots pine woodland, moors, peat and bog, some crofting land, and the two lochs (Garten and Mallachie). Within these habitats is found a great diversity of birds, plants, animals and insects.

Having watched the ospreys for some time, we decided to go on a guided walk, led by the assistant warden, which took us along the shore of Loch Garten and through woodland to the northern edge of Loch Mallachie. We are not, on the whole, keen on tramping through reserves en masse, but this walk was an exception. We thoroughly enjoyed it, learning more in under three hours from our excellent guide than we could have by ourselves in three weeks.

Our attention was drawn first of all to the area of ancient pine forest, easily distinguished from more recent plantations we saw later on by the immense diversity of shape, size and age of the pine trees, and the thick ground cover of such typical plants as juniper and bilberry. In the short walk along the road before we turned off down the side of the loch there were a number of other plants such as marsh thistle, cow-wheat, lady's bedstraw, spear thistle and the fairly localised creeping lady's tresses. We saw a Scotch Argus butterfly – just one of about eighteen species recorded, and also caught sight of a common sandpiper as it took off from the rocky water's edge and flicked across the loch. Some of the loch's roost of about 3,000 black-headed gulls were being their usual noisy selves. Breeding populations of teal, tufted ducks, mallard and wigeons are usually present, and in winter, upwards of a thousand greylag geese roost on Garten at night, and feed in the area by day.

As we turned off the road and wandered along the well-defined paths through the wood, we noted the comparative starkness of the newer stands of Scots pine – much more regimented than the ancient Caledonian remnants, with a less diverse understorey. On one side of the track was an area which was being partially cleared to allow more diverse growth, regeneration, and some planting; but great care was being taken to leave plenty of old logs and stumps, as these are the nesting sites for the rare crested tit – the reserve having, on average, about twenty pairs. It was a great thrill to see a number of these enchanting little birds at close quarters. We also had a stroke of good fortune in seeing and hearing a small flock of another of the reserve's nesting specialities – Scottish crossbills. These, the only species of bird actually indigenous to Britain, are now recognised as a separate species (*Loxia scotica*) from the common crossbill of Europe (*Loxia curvirostra*) by reason of bill size difference and of reproductive isolation. Feeding almost exclusively on pine seeds extracted by the crossed mandibles, the red male and the yellow-green female also nest in their food trees, lining the twig structure with grasses.

Also present in the woods were coal tits, the occasional willow

On our guided walk some of the loch's roost of 3,000 black-headed gulls were being their usual noisy selves.

warbler and some spotted flycatchers – but we saw none of the siskins which are often present, or the capercaillies which also breed on the reserve. We paused for some time on the edge of the smaller Loch Mallachie, watching a heron and admiring through our binoculars the profuse growth of white waterlilies on the opposite bank and fringing the small island some distance off shore.

The Insh Marshes RSPB Reserve

Managing body   RSPB.
Access   NH 7799. South side of A9 Kingussie – Boat of Garten road, between B970 and River Spey.
Other information   Reception centre. Leaflet. Hides. Summer opening, restricted days. Winter visits by arrangement with warden: Ivy Cottage, Insh, Kingussie, Inverness-shire.

To judge the Insh Marshes reserve on what we saw when we visited it would be to do it a grave injustice. We had one of those awful days which come to all birdwatchers occasionally – an almost total blank, with just a few waders, some wildfowl and some rather commonplace passerines. To be fair, we had timed our visit to Speyside to see the ospreys at nearby Loch Garten to the greatest advantage, and that happened to be in late July when the marshes are at their quietest. Nevertheless, the Insh Marshes at almost any other time of the year have much to offer. The varied habitats contain good populations, not just of birds, but of mammals, insects and amphibians, as well as a diversity of plants including some national rarities.

The reserve consists of extensive marshes lying in the floodplain of the Spey, guarded to the west by the Monadhiath Mountains and to the east by the spectacular Cairngorms. The largest habitat within the reserve is sedge fen, containing tracts of the very local northern water sedge (*Carex aquatilis*) and some other sedges, which are a major food resource for the wintering wildfowl. Bordering the marshland area are large banks of willow carr, often with sedge understorey, and with the delightfully scented bog myrtle growing in profusion at its edge. The river is fringed by willow, alder and some bird cherry. Throughout the reserve is a network of ditches – relics of former unsuccessful attempts to drain the plain, and there are also a number of permanent pools. These support a wealth of plant and animal life. Bog bean, bulrush, waterlilies and yellow iris are common, and the rare least iris is found in the ditches together with the local greater bladderwort. There are some stands of mature birchwood, with juniper understorey, and several small

The woodland areas around the Insh Marshes hold a good variety of small birds, including redpolls.

conifer woods, both of which provide shelter for small birds.

The whole area of the floodplain from Loch Insh near Kincraig to Kingussie some five miles distant is liable to flooding up to depths of eight feet. The marshes are of international importance as during the winter they support about 200 whooper swans, and in contrast to many other sites the swans are able to enjoy natural foodstuffs such as water plants and seeds. The number of whoopers represents ten per cent of the entire British wintering population, and about one per cent of the European population. Other wintering birds include both greylag and white-fronted geese, shovelers, wigeons, pintails, teal, mallard and goosanders. Mallard, teal, tufted ducks and red-breasted mergansers breed here (the latter only occasionally). Breeding waders include curlews, lapwings, redshanks, snipe and, a rare occurrence in Britain, the wood sandpiper. Two birds which are rarely seen can however be heard – water rails quite frequently (four pairs breed) and the spotted crake less often.

The Insh Marshes are an excellent place for seeing birds of prey. Buzzards breed regularly, and there is a communal roost of hen harriers in winter, spring and autumn of up to ten birds. Marsh harriers are less common visitors, as are peregrines, merlins and kestrels. Ospreys from Loch Garten are seen during the summer, fishing the Spey and the pools. While we were there, someone thought they glimpsed one disappearing behind the hide, but by the time we had all rushed out, it had vanished over the hills.

The woodland areas hold a variety of small birds such as willow warblers, tree-creepers, tits, redpolls and a few flycatchers. Marsh birds include reed buntings, marsh warblers, a few grasshopper warblers and meadow pipits. A famous year for the reserve was 1968, when a blue throat female and a nest with eggs was found – the only known British nesting attempt – but, tragically, the nest was predated.

In spite of the proximity of the mountains, red deer are rarely seen on the marshes, although roe are quite common. They live deep in the marsh and, when flooding occurs, they are seen swimming between the islands of higher, drier ground. Badgers, stoats and foxes are present in the woods, and rabbits provide welcome food for birds of prey, such as buzzards. There are plenty of fish in the river – it is famous for salmon and brown and sea trout – trout being the principal food of the ospreys. On the marsh, pike are common, as are eels.

If planning a visit to the Insh Marshes, it is certainly essential to take account of the time of the year, and to establish when the hides are open. April, May and June are the best spring and summer months, while July and August are best for birds of prey. Obviously the wintering wildfowl are worth seeing, from November to March, unless the weather is very severe, when most of the birds will move away. Access to the reserve is limited to the hides and connecting walks.

Ben More Coigach and Inverpolly

Managing body (Ben More Coigach)   Scottish Wildlife Trust/Royal Society
for Nature Conservation.
Access   NC 0807 (others also). Best seen from Drumrunie – Achiltibuie
road and from coastal road along the shore of Loch Broom from Achiltibuie
to Culnocraig.
Managing body (Inverpolly)   NCC.
Access   NC 1312. Knockan Cliff nature trail (NC 1909) on A835 north of
Ullapool.
Other information   Information centre at Knockan.

If we could return to just one reserve of all those we have visited,
the choice would be easy – it would be Inverpolly National Nature
Reserve in the north-west Highlands. A close runner-up would be
its near neighbour, Ben More Coigach, managed by the Scottish
Wildlife Trust. They both lie between Ullapool and Lochinver and
encompass what is to us some of the most magical and compelling
country that we have seen in the whole of Britain. As they are so
close, and because the wildlife that may be found in one is virtually
the same as that in the other, it seems logical to describe them both
in the same chapter.

Our visit to the reserves began well, because on our first morning
the first thing we saw was a single seal, only a short distance out to
sea. It was surfacing and diving, and we quickly realised it was also
feeding, as it came up with a very large salmon in its jaws – we
could see the pink flesh quite plainly. The local seagulls were flying
low over it, hoping for any scraps that were dropped from the seal's
mouth. We watched for quite some time before it eventually
disappeared out to sea.

Ben More Coigach is a large reserve, although at 14,600 acres only
about half the size of Inverpolly, and extends from the town of
Achiltibuie overlooking the famous Summer Isles in the south, to
the lochs Lurgainn, Bad a 'Ghaill and Osgaig in the north, and
includes the 2,438 foot peak of Ben More. The fringes of the reserve
can be seen from the Drumrunie to Achiltibuie single-track road,
from which some wonderful views are obtained. The road runs
through rough, rugged country, with high peaks towering over it
much of the way, and over the lochs which run beside it for almost
half its length.

It was along this road that we had one of our greatest pieces of
good fortune. We parked and climbed up a steep rock-encrusted
mountainside, stopping from time to time to admire the panorama
spread out below and opposite – mountain peaks as far as the eye

could see one minute, and hidden from us the next as we were enveloped in swirling mist and cloud. As we rested, about two-thirds of the way from the top, we looked down on the loch below. Suddenly, we saw on a very small lochan several birds with the outline of divers, but from that height we could not be sure which one. There were three of them swimming back and forth, disappearing from time to time as they submerged. We rushed down the mountainside, then slowly and carefully edged our way forward until we came within about twenty-five yards of the water, slightly below the level of the reeds fringing it. Very cautiously, we raised our heads and peered through the vegetation. There, sitting quietly on the water, was a magnificent black-throated diver in full breeding plumage. He was a superb sight and, as we watched, he dived and re-appeared again a little distance away before eventually vanishing among the vegetation on the far side of the water. Of the other two birds we had seen from the mountain there was no sign, but it did seem as if we had chanced upon a little family party of the divers, of which there are all too few in the Highlands – the total British breeding population is only about 200 pairs. As a bonus, while we were sitting by the shore of the loch, a small party of greylag geese went sailing past. They, too, nest on the reserve.

We drove on towards Achiltibuie, and everywhere along the way we saw wheatears – on the walls, among the heather and in the fields. We enjoyed the view out across the bay to the Summer Isles, and then our gaze turned towards the hills once more, where we saw a large party of big black birds wheeling, circling and diving around the rocky crags at the summit of one of the hills. We were sure we knew what they were but we wanted a closer view, so we set off up the hillside, more gentle this time, and although rocky outcrops were scattered about the going was much easier. Little areas of bog with sphagnum moss and purple moor grass nestled below the rocks, but much of the vegetation consisted of thick patches of long heather. As we climbed, the flock of birds became more clearly visible, and in addition to their acrobatic tumbling and wheeling, their distinctively-shaped tails and their raucous, gutteral calls confirmed our original belief that they were ravens. They were a delight to watch, as they disappeared behind the rocky summit, then came flying back, tumbling, turning and gliding – resting on the cliff edges before taking off again for a repeat performance. The strange acoustics somehow ensured that the closer we came to the birds, the less we could hear them.

As we walked back down the hill, a medium-sized brown bird flew quickly past us and landed on a rock about twenty-five yards away. Briefly, we thought it was a raptor of some sort, until we had a better view and saw the white patch at the back of its neck, and

As we drove towards Achiltibuie we saw wheatears everywhere – on the walls, among the heather, and in the fields.

then as it turned, the startling red lining of its open mouth. It was a young cuckoo. We immediately looked round for the foster parent and soon saw a meadow pipit on another rock. It was looking nervously around, and had an insect in its beak. Sure enough after hesitating a little longer, it flew over to its monster foster-child and thrust the insect into the wide gape – almost disappearing within it as it did so. It made several trips, each time bringing more food. Then the cuckoo flew off and out of our view.

We saw only a tiny fraction of what the Ben More Coigach reserve has to offer, but enough, as so often, to whet our appetite for more. The range of habitats is typical of the West Highlands – the two major peaks of Ben More and Beinn an Eoin, dominate the reserve; there are acres upon acres of heather moorland, bogs with bog asphodel and sundews, woodlands consisting mostly of birch with aspen, holly and rowan, and, as might be expected, both plant and animal life abounds.

Ferns are plentiful – northern buckler fern, brittle bladder fern to name but two – and the mosses, lichens and liverworts are in their element in the damp environment. Breeding birds include the peregrine, raven, golden eagle, ring ouzel, greenshank, twite and ptarmigan. There are red deer in their hundreds and smaller numbers of pine martens, otters and wild cats. But the visitor to this

167

vast reserve and its even vaster neighbour, Inverpolly, will be disappointed if they expect to see a great deal in a short time; these are two of the last great wildernesses of the British Isles.

Inverpolly covers an area of nearly 27,000 acres, the second largest National Nature Reserve in the country, and its habitats include lochs, bogs, seashore, marine islands, beaches, hazel and rowan woodlands, scree and high mountains with the 2,800 foot high Cul Mor towering over it all.

Leaflets may be obtained from the visitor centre at Knockan, describing the adjoining signposted walks; one the Knockan Cliff nature trail, and the other, covering some of the same ground, the Knockan Cliff geological trail.

We decided to follow the nature trail, which winds its way up the very steep and rugged cliff-face. Although it is not noted for the birds seen on or near it, the trail is none the less instructive. It makes some interesting points about the general natural history of the area, and shows how the habitats have been built up over thousands of years to the climax of mixed forest vegetation which was typical up to about 4,000 years ago.

The first stopping place on the trail drew our attention to the lichens on the rocks – a feature throughout the trail and the reserve as a whole – and described the role they play in soil formation. Looking across to the loch on the far side of the road, we saw a sight that was to become increasingly familiar throughout our stay in the Highlands – a red-throated diver. We had seen these occasionally around the coast at reserves in England, but there was something very special about seeing them in what one feels is their natural habitat. Black-throated divers can also be seen from the trail.

The next stop was to examine some mosses, and again the leaflet described the part they play in soil formation by trapping moisture which, in the winter, freezes and helps to crack the rock and so break it down. They also exude chemicals which assist that process further. We admired the fine example of Polytrichum moss, but it was later, when we ventured off the trail and into the hills that the mosses really came into their own.

Further up the trail, we were immediately below a large area of scree, and we could see how this slope was gradually being covered with vegetation. At about this level too, some of the delightful wild flowers were in evidence, such as yellow saxifrage and alpine lady's mantle. A little further on, a few rowan trees were clinging to the side of the cliff – remnants of the forest of Scots pine, birch and rowan that would have covered the area thousands of years ago. Today, the rowan berries provide winter food for birds such as fieldfares and redwings. The leaflet explains that with a change to a much wetter climate 4,000 years ago, the growth of sphagnum moss under the trees increased dramatically, with a subsequent build-up, over many centuries, of peat – much in evidence in this area. This restricted the regeneration of the pine forest, so it began to die out, and at a later date, the remainder was felled for firewood by man. In this area, there were also some smaller birds hopping about – chiefly wheatears and pipits, and the occasional robin.

At this stage, the leaflet warns that the trail becomes steeper and more exposed. 'So take great care and turn back if the winds are too strong or if you do not feel confident about continuing'. We decided to go on and, after quite a strenuous climb, reached a kind of semi-summit, and the safety of a raised wooden walkway. From this vantage point we had breath-taking views across to the cloud-enveloped peaks of Cul Mor and Cul Beag. Much of the top of the cliff is heather moorland, the home of the red grouse which feeds on heather shoots and crowberry. We followed the pathway down to the far end of the trail, past an extraordinary old tree root by the side of the track – a remnant of the old Caledonian pine forest and about 4,000 years old.

The geological trail is of great interest, as Knockan Cliff played a vital part in the history and understanding of geology, showing as it does that huge masses of rock can, due to underground forces, slide up a fault line and end up on top of rock that is actually much younger.

In the afternoon, we drove round the margins of the reserve to Lochinver, and then back into it on the coastline at Enard Bay, where we saw a number of sea ducks and mergansers, as well as one or two rock pipits on the shore. On the way back, we passed a whole series of lochs, and a surprising number had red-throated divers on them.

The next day turned out to be probably the most memorable of our Scottish visit. We returned to the visitor centre at Knockan and instead of following the nature trail again, we crossed the main road and followed a pathway that led up into the hills towards Drumrunie Forest. Within a quarter of an hour we were out of sight and sound of the road – and we had entered another world. We were surrounded by heather and deer sedge covered hills, often rock-peaked, and as we breasted each rise another magnificent vista opened up before us – lochs, glens and mountain peaks. The weather deteriorated, and a fine, misty rain swept across, hiding the views, then revealing them again – each one beautiful, remote and utterly unspoilt. In spite of the rain, the colours all around us were incredible – the varying shades of the sphagnum moss in the boggy areas ranging from the brightest of greens through rusty brown to deep red. The rocks themselves were covered in delicate mosaics of greens, fawns and yellows, and the red and green of the sundews with their creamy-white flowers added contrast to the minute rock gardens that seemed to be enclosed in so many of the hollows at the foot of each miniature crag. We walked on, almost overwhelmed by the beauty of this marvellous country.

We saw a few wheatears – but as we reached the summit of every rise there was always the possibility that we might see a golden eagle circling over one of the peaks, put up some grouse from the heather, or glimpse a ptarmigan – all of which are on the reserve. Although we did not see any of the 500 or so red deer, there were plenty of signs of them – fresh slots that told us they were not far away. Nor did we see any other human beings.

There is a wealth of wildlife at Inverpolly, but the place is so huge and remote that it is not always obvious. Birds, in addition to those already mentioned, include red-breasted mergansers, whooper swans, kestrels, buzzards, ringed and golden plovers, hooded crows, ring ouzels, goosanders, barnacle geese, ravens and a range of woodland birds such as wood warblers, long-tailed tits, long-eared owls and spotted flycatchers; while the coastal areas offer sightings of black guillimots, fulmars and shags. Among the mammals are otters, badgers, wild cats and pine martens.

Of the plants, ferns grow everywhere – with Wilson's filmy fern and lemon-scented fern common in places, a considerable variety of bryophytes, and wild flowers in abundance – meadow-sweet, melancholy thistle, self-heal, bog bean, lesser bladderwort – in all, nearly 400 species. A lifetime could be spent on this reserve without seeing all it has to offer.

Other Reserves in Great Britain

South-east England

AMBERLEY WILD BROOKS
Managing Body Sussex Trust for Nature Conservation.
Access TQ 0315. Park in Amberley village on north side of B2139, 3 miles SW of Storrington. Reserve reached by public footpath from village.
Habitat Flooded meadows.
Birds Wintering Bewick's swan, teal, wigeon, pintail, shoveler.

ARLINGTON RESERVOIR
Managing body East Sussex County Council.
Access TQ 5307. NE of Eastbourne along A27. Take road to Berwick. Reservoir is just north of Berwick station.
Habitat Reservoir.
Birds Wildfowl including Canada goose, mallard, tufted duck, shoveler, wigeon.

ARUNDEL WILDFOWL TRUST
Managing body The Wildfowl Trust.
Access TQ 0208. Signposted from Arundel.
Habitat Reed-beds, open path, grassland.
Birds Ducks, kingfisher, green sandpiper, water rail, Cetti's warbler.

BURHAM MARSH
Managing body Kent Trust for Nature Conservation.
Access TQ 7162.
Habitat Reed-beds, marsh, river.
Birds Wetland species and migrants.

BOUGH BEECHES
Managing body Kent Trust for Nature Conservation.
Access TQ 4949.
Habitat Lake and reservoir.
Birds Migrants, garganey, common scoter, osprey on passage, waders, spotted sandpiper, redneck phalarope, wintering wildfowl.

BROXHEAD COMMON
Managing body Hampshire County Council.
Access SU 8137.
Habitat Heathland, birch and pine.
Birds Tree pipit, redpoll, whitethroat.

BURTON POND
Managing body   West Sussex County Council/Sussex Trust for Nature Conservation.
Access   SU 9818.
Habitat   Lake, heath, bog, woodland.
Birds   Pochard, water rail, reed and sedge warblers, teal, tufted duck, great crested grebe, little grebe.
Other information   Leaflet from West Sussex County Council.

CASTLE HILL
Managing body   NCC.
Access   TQ 3707.
Habitat   Chalk grassland.
Birds   Linnet, whitethroat, yellowhammer, corn bunting, meadow pipit.

THE CHASE, WOOLTON HILL
Managing body   Hampshire & Isle of Wight Naturalists' Trust.
Access   SU 4463.   Access from minor road Woolton Hill to Woodhay station.
Habitat   Conifer woodland, lake, alder carr, mixed woodland.
Birds   Kingfisher, siskin, redpoll, woodpeckers, wood warbler.

CRABWOOD
Managing body   Hampshire & Isle of Wight Naturalists' Trust/Hampshire County Council.
Access   SU 4430. On minor road from Standen to Sparsholt, approximately 1 mile south of Sparsholt.
Habitat   Old oak and hazel woodland, beech, ash, aspen.
Birds   Nightjar, nightingale, woodpeckers and common woodland species.

CUCKMERE HAVEN
Managing body   East Sussex County Council/Lewes District Council.
Access   TV 5299.
Habitat   Downland, cliffs, estuary.
Birds   Little grebe, teal, tufted duck, wigeon, heron, shelduck, ring ouzel, pied flycatcher, common and lesser whitethroats, blackcap, grasshopper and willow warblers, stonechat, redstart, jackdaw, fulmar.

CURBRIDGE
Managing body   Hampshire & Isle of Wight Naturalists' Trust.
Access   SU 5312. Take A3051 Botley – Fareham road to Horse & Jockey public house car-park at Curbridge.
Habitat   Salt marsh, freshwater marsh and woodland adjoining river and creek.
Birds   Over 70 species of woodland and wetland birds.

ELMLEY MARSHES
Managing body   RSPB.
Access   TQ 9470. One mile from Kingferry on Sheerness road, signposted.
Habitat   Grazing marshes, freshwater fleets, shallow floods, salt marshes, mud-flats.
Birds   Teal, mallard, wigeon, shelduck, white-fronted goose, black-tailed godwit, curlew, dunlin, redshank. Breeding birds – redshank, lapwing,

pochard, common tern. Resident short-eared owl, wintering hen harrier, merlin. Waders on passage.
Other information   Facilities for elderly and disabled.

FLEET POND
Managing body   Hart District Council.
Access   SU 8255.
Habitat   Heath, woodland, open water.
Birds   Canada goose, great crested grebe, rarities such as great reed warbler and blue-winged teal.

HIGH HALSTOW MARSHES
Managing body   NCC.
Access   TQ 8076.
Habitat   Salt marsh, mud-flats.
Birds   Gadwall, shoveler, teal, garganey, pochard, pintail, shelduck, white-fronted goose, curlew, grey and golden plovers, redshank, heron, knot, dunlin.

HOOK
Managing body   Hampshire County Council.
Access   SU 4906.
Habitat   Estuary, mud-flats, saltmarsh, wet meadows, freshwater marsh, woodland.
Birds   Winter – wildfowl and waders. Summer – sedge warbler, yellow-hammer, stonechat.

KEYHAVEN – PENNINGTON MARSHES
Managing body   Hampshire & Isle of Wight Naturalists' Trust.
Access   SZ 3191. Parking in Keyhaven village for access to sea-wall. No access off rights of way.
Habitat   Mud-flats, salt marsh, shingle, brackish ditches, lagoons, scrub, woodland.
Birds   Little, common and Sandwich terns, brent goose, red-throated diver, common scoter, Arctic and great skuas, little gull, black tern, godwits, green and spotted redshanks, ruff, little stint, whimbrel.

KILN WOOD
Managing body   Kent Trust for Nature Conservation.
Access   TQ 8951.
Habitat   Coppiced woodland and pond.
Birds   Woodland species including nightingale, warblers, kingfisher, nuthatch, tree-creeper.

LANGSTONE HARBOUR
Managing body   RSPB.
Access   SU 6806. West of A3023 between South Hayling and the A27 Chichester – Fareham road. No access, but may be viewed from coastal path.
Habitat   Estuary, mud-flats, creeks, salt marsh islands.
Birds   Waders, wildfowl, breeding little grebe, moorhen, coot, snipe and Jack snipe. Summer nesting – whitethroats, blackcap and willow warbler. Winter – bearded tit, dark-bellied brent goose, black-necked grebe, red-breasted merganser, goldeneye.

LOWER TEST VALLEY
Managing body   Hampshire & Isle of Wight Naturalists' Trust.
Access   SU 3615. West of Southampton. Access over level crossing opposite new lorry park entrance south of roundabout off M275 to Nursling Industrial Estate. Access by public footpaths only.
Habitat   Reed-beds, water meadows, brackish water, grassland, salt marsh.
Birds   Redshank, snipe, little grebe, warblers, wigeon, sandpipers, water pipit, bearded tit, redpoll, siskin, waders.

NORTHWOOD HILL
Managing body   RSPB.
Access   TQ 7876. Near village of High Halstow, north of A228 Rochester – Grain road.
Habitat   Oak woodland, scrub, hawthorn thickets.
Birds   Britain's largest heronry, turtle dove, nightingale, whitethroat, lesser whitethroat, blackcap, garden warbler.

SANDWICH BAY
Managing body   Kent Trust for Nature Conservation/RSPB/NT.
Access   TR 3562. A256 north of Sandwich, through Sandwich Bay estate. Cars as far as Prince's Gold Clubhouse, then on foot along beach. Toll.
Habitat   Grassland, dunes, beach, foreshore, salt marsh
Birds   Roosting and feeding wildfowl and waders, winter divers, hen harriers, snow bunting.

SOUTH SWALE
Managing body   Kent Trust for Nature Conservation.
Access   TR 0365. Park near Old Sportsman Inn. Walk along public footpath following sea-wall.
Habitat   Beach, foreshore, tidal mud-flats.
Birds   Dark-bellied brent goose, wigeon, waders, migrants, shore lark, snow bunting.
Other information   Permit off rights of way.

TITCHFIELD HAVEN
Managing body   Hampshire County Council/Hampshire & Isle of Wight Naturalists' Trust.
Access   SU 5302. Permit required.
Habitat   River bank, reed-beds, marsh field.
Birds   Winter – ducks and waders. Summer – reed, sedge and grasshopper warblers, terns, hobby, grebes, brent goose.

WALTHAM BROOKS
Managing body   Sussex Trust for Nature Conservation.
Access   TQ 0316. Reserve on south side of minor road from Coldwaltham to Greatham Bridge, 2 miles SW of Pulborough off A29. Public footpath along side of old canal running across reserve.
Habitat   Flood meadows.
Birds   Wildfowl including gadwall, shoveler, teal, wigeon, Bewick's swan. Some waders including redshank.

WOODS MILL
Managing body   HQ of Sussex Trust for Nature Conservation.
Access   TQ 2214. On A2037 1½ miles south of Henfield
Habitat   Lake, marsh, woodland, grassland, water garden.
Birds   Kingfisher, wren, willow warbler, goldfinch, siskin, redpoll, fieldfare, reed bunting, sedge warbler, tits.

South-west England

AYLESBEARE COMMON
Managing body   RSPB.
Access   SY 0690. North of A3032 Lyme Regis – Exeter road, 2 miles west of Newton Poppleford.
Habitat   Dry and wet heathland with valley bog and streams, deciduous woodland and alder scrub.
Birds   Nightjar, stonechat, yellowhammer, curlew, Dartford warbler, tree pipit, marsh tit, woodpeckers.

BERRY HEAD COUNTRY PARK
Managing body   Torbay Borough Council.
Access   SX 9556. Signposted from Brixham town centre.
Habitat   Heathland-topped headland.
Birds   One of few south coast colonies of auks – guillimots and razorbills. Also fulmar, kittiwake, jackdaw, cormorant, gannet, linnet, stonechat, black redstart, buzzard, kestrel.

BOVEY VALLEY WOODLANDS
Managing body   NCC.
Access   SX 7980.
Habitat   Old coppiced hazel and oak woodland.
Birds   Pied flycatcher, redstart, wood warbler, dipper, wagtail.
Other information   Permit off rights of way.

BUDE MARSHES
Managing body   North Cornwall District Council.
Access   SS 2106.
Habitat   Coastal marshland.
Birds   Autumn migrants, breeding reed and sedge warblers, visiting heron and kestrel.
Other information   Hide available.

DART VALLEY
Managing body   Devon Trust for Nature Conservation/Dartmoor National Parks.
Access   SX 6773 (northern end). SX 7170 (southern end). For northern end, car-park at Dartmeet, cross A384, reserve on both sides of river. Southern end, park at Newbridge and walk along track on north side of river. Other access points marked between Dartmeet and Newbridge on A384.
Habitat   Moorland and typical pedunculate/sessile oak Dartmoor woodland, riverside marsh, valley bogs.
Birds   Dipper, grey wagtail, buzzard, raven, woodcock, marsh tit, green woodpecker, redstart, meadow pipit, ring ouzel, goldcrest, long-tailed tit.

EXE ESTUARY
Managing body   Various owners/managers.
Access   Exmouth: Imperial car-park – turn right beside bus and rail station, continue past Sports Centre. For mudbanks, take Exeter road, turn left after Gypsy Lane traffic lights into Belle Vue Road, then right into Halsdon Avenue, which leads to river. For pier, access from Victoria Road, or far end of esplanade.
The Villages: Cockwood & Starcross – on A379 to Dawlish from A38 Exeter by-pass; Lympstone – on A377 Exeter/Exmouth road; Exton – also on A377, turn right at signpost to 'Puffing Billy Inn'. Park beside railway halt; Powderham – from A379 take turning towards Powderham Church 1 mile south of Exminster.
Exminster Marshes: from A379 towards Dawlish take left fork after Exminster village signposted 'Swan's Nest'. Parking at end of track; Topsham – car-parks or by recreation ground; Bowling Green Marsh – take A377 towards Exmouth, turning right before reaching River Clyst; Countess Wear – parking on south side of old Exeter by-pass between river and canal. Footpath towards Topsham.
Habitat   Huge area of open water, sand, mud-flats, salt marsh, river.
Birds   Waders and wildfowl, avocets.

PURBECK MARINE RESERVE INCLUDING PURBECK CLIFFS
Managing body   Dorset Naturalists' Trust.
Access   SZ 0378. On foot from Swanage and Durlstone Head. Kimmeridge Bay.
Habitat   Limestone cliffs.
Birds   Puffin, fulmar, razorbill, guillimot, kittiwakes. Black redstart in winter.

RED MOOR
Managing body   Cornwall Trust for Nature Conservation.
Access   SX 0762. Turn left off B3269 Bodmin – Lostwithiel road about 2 miles from Bodmin. Follow road past Little Tredinnick Farm, then south at junction and park at triangle junction. Entrance up lane leading west.
Habitat   Wetland, open water, willow carr, scrub.
Birds   Nightjar, linnet, yellowhammer, stonechat.
Other information   Permit required.

SLAPTON LEY
Managing body   Field Studies Council.
Access   SX 8343.
Habitat   Shingle, freshwater lagoon, reed-beds, mixed woodlands.
Birds   Over 200 species recorded. Great crested grebe, water rail, Cetti's and grasshopper warblers, stonechat, goldcrest. Nesting nearby – fulmar and greater black-backed gull.
Other information   Permit for woodlands and Higher Ley from South Hams Countryside Unit, Slapton Ley Field Centre, Slapton, Devon.

STANPIT MARSH
Managing body   Christchurch Borough Council.
Access   SZ 1792. From car-park in Stanpit lane, Christchurch.
Habitat   Estuary, mud-flats, salt and freshwater marshes, reed-beds, scrub.
Birds   Passage wildfowl and waders, little tern, bearded tit.

Central England

BLAKENEY POINT
Managing body NT.
Access TG 0046. By boat from Morston or Blakeney Quays, or on foot (3½ miles of shingle) from Cley Beach.
Habitat Shingle spit, dunes, salt marsh.
Birds Breeding common, little and Sandwich terns, autumn migrants, waders, winter ducks. Dark-bellied brents.

BRADFIELD WOODS
Managing body Suffolk Trust for Nature Conservation.
Access TL 9358.
Habitat Coppice woodland.
Birds Willow and garden warblers, blackcap, nightingale, woodcock, woodpeckers, tawny owl, brambling, redpoll.
Other information Permit off pathways.

EAST WRETHAM HEATH
Managing body Norfolk Naturalists' Trust.
Access TL 9188. Contact warden's office (10.00 or 14.00) at NE corner of reserve about 5 miles NE of Thetford on A1075, which leaves A11 2 miles from Thetford.
Habitat Breckland heath, meres, pine woodland.
Birds Crossbill, long-eared owl, hawfinch, hen harrier, stone curlew, nightjar, stonechat, wheatear, red-backed shrike.
Other information Permit required other than along Drove road.

ELY – ROSWELL PITS
Managing body Anglian Water Authority.
Access TL 5580.
Habitat Meadow, scrub, woodland, flooded clay workings.
Birds Breeding great crested grebe, shoveler, reed and sedge warblers, redpoll, blackcap, wintering pochard, tufted duck, goldeneye, Slavonian grebe. Passage greenshank, black-tailed godwit, ruff. Occasional black common and little terns.

FOWLMERE
Managing body RSPB.
Access TL 4146. Off main Cambridge – Royston A10. Turn off Shepreth – Fowlmere road by cemetery and park off road.
Habitat Fen, arable farmland, reed-swamp, mere, hawthorn scrub and alderwood, river.
Birds Reed, sedge and grasshopper warblers, reed bunting, water rail, kingfisher, whitethroat, lesser whitethroat, blackcap, turtle dove, spotted flycatcher, fieldfare, redwing, corn bunting, pied wagtail, greenshank.

HAVERGATE ISLAND
Managing body RSPB.
Access TM 4250. Take A12 from Ipswich – Woodbridge, then right onto B1084 to Orford Quay. By boat from Orford Quay.
Habitat Shallow lagoons with island, salt marsh, shingle beaches.

Birds Biggest avocet colony, Sandwich tern, oystercatcher, ringed plover, redshank, passage waders, wintering duck.
Other information Permits by written application in advance. Warden: 30 Mundays Lane, Orford, Woodbridge.

HAYLEY WOOD
Managing body Cambridgeshire and Isle of Ely Naturalists' Trust – Cambient.
Access TL 2954. Pedestrian access only along Hayley Lane off B1046 St Neots – Barton road, 1¾ miles west of junction with A14 at Longstowe, opposite large water-tower.
Habitat Mixed woodland on clay.
Birds Woodpeckers, tree creeper, long-tailed, marsh and willow tits, linnet, redpoll, warblers, redwing, fieldfare.
Other information Permit. Trail guides.

HOLME DUNES
Managing body Norfolk Naturalists' Trust.
Access TF 7145. Take Holme Beach road north from A149 Hunstanton – Wells road, 3 miles NE of Hunstanton. Just before golf course, turn right along track to main gate; or walk along Thornham sea-wall.
Habitat Foreshore, dunes, salt marsh, freshwater marsh.
Birds Water rail, green sandpiper, spotted redshank, greenshank, snow bunting, shore lark, warblers, marsh harrier, great skua.
Other information: Permit from warden; The Firs, Broadwater Road, Holme-next-the-Sea (Holme 240).

LANDGUARD
Managing body Suffolk Trust for Nature Conservation/Suffolk County Council.
Access TM 2832. Via Langer and Carr Roads, Felixstowe, Turn left into private road signposted 'Dock Viewing Area'. Reserve between Landguard Forest and sea.
Habitat Shingle. scrub, woodland.
Birds Little tern, ringed plover, wheatear, black redstart, shelduck, linnet, red-legged partridge, warblers.

LONG MYND
Managing body NT.
Access SO 4294.
Habitat Moorland, stream.
Birds Grouse, dipper, yellowhammer, wheatear, ring ouzel, buzzard, raven.

MARTHAM BROAD
Managing body Norfolk Naturalists' Trust.
Access TG 4518. May be viewed from 2 public footpaths, one from West Somerton round the south side, the other on NE bank of river past old mill at West Somerton.
Habitat Wet alder woodland, water, reed-beds, sedge beds.
Birds Great crested grebe, tufted duck, common tern, bearded tit, bittern, marsh harrier, wintering ducks.

NORTH WARREN
Managing body RSPB.
Access TM 4559. Entrance to car-park between houses off Aldeburgh – Leiston road.
Habitat Grass heathland, fen, mixed woodland, farmland, disused railway.
Birds Yellowhammer, linnet, nightingale, garden warbler, whitethroat, lesser whitethroat, wheatear, finches, thrushes, reed, sedge and grasshopper warblers, kingfisher, bearded tit.

STRUMPSHAW FEN
Managing body RSPB.
Access TG 3406. From A47 Great Yarmouth to Brundall, turn sharp right into Low Road; car-park by railway. Entrance across level crossing.
Habitat Fen, reed-swamp, alder and willow carr, damp woodland, grazing marshes, open water.
Birds Marsh harrier, bearded tit, Cetti's warbler, water rail, great crested grebe, redshank, woodpeckers, bean geese, wildfowl, great grey shrike.

WALBERSWICK
Managing body NCC.
Access TM 4773. Good views from B1387 and from lane west from Walberswick towards Westwood Lodge. Elsewhere keep to public pathways.
Habitat Woodland, heath, reed-beds, mud-flats, tidal estuary, freshwater marsh.
Birds Marsh harrier, bearded tit, water rail, bittern, nightjar, wintering spotted redshank, passage and winter wildfowl, waders, raptors.
Other information Permit off rights of way.

WICKEN FEN
Managing body NT.
Access TL 5670. South of A1123, 3 miles SW of Soham.
Habitat Open water, reed-beds, wet meadows, scrub.
Birds Snipe, woodcock, redshank, long-eared owl, wintering wildfowl, hen harrier roost, bittern, great grey shrike.
Other information Open daily by permit or National Trust card.

WINTERTON DUNES
Managing body NCC.
Access TG 5020.
Habitat Sand, shingle, acid dunes, damp slacks, grazing marsh.
Birds Brambling, redpoll, siskin, fieldfare, redwing, hen harrier, buzzard, chiffchaff, warblers, little tern.

WOLVES WOOD
Managing body RSPB.
Access TM 0544. Entrance off A1071 Ipswich road 2 miles east of Hadleigh.
Habitat Mixed broad-leaved woodland, coppiced scrub.
Birds Nightingale, garden warbler, blackcap, whitethroat, chiffchaff, willow warbler, woodcock, hawfinch, tits, nuthatch, woodpeckers.

179

Wales

BOSHERTON POOLS
Managing body   NT/NCC.
Access   SR 9795. B4319 for 5 miles. Turn left on to minor road to Bosherton. Car-park in village.
Habitat   Fish ponds, dunes, cliffs.
Birds   Sea-birds, pochard, goldeneye, gadwall, grebes, kingfisher, red-breasted merganser, smew, heron, teal.

CADER IDRIS
Managing body   NCC.
Access   SH 7311. Three miles SW of Dolgellau.
Habitat   Lake, mixed woodland, mountain range, cliffs, heath.
Birds   Breeding raven, wheatear, ring ouzel, pied flycatcher.
Other information   Permit for enclosed woodland.

COED-Y-BEDW
Managing body   Glamorgan Naturalists' Trust.
Access   ST 1283. Stile at Forestry Commission nameboard on north side of road from Morganstown to Pentyrch.
Habitat   Valley woodland, sessile oak, birch, stream.
Birds   Tree pipit, wood warbler, pied flycatcher, redstart, woodpeckers, grey wagtail, woodcock.

COED-Y-CASTELL
Managing body   Brecon Beacons National Parks.
Access   SN 6819.
Habitat   Oak, ash and hazel woodland.
Birds   Wood warbler, raven, buzzard, pied flycatcher.

COEDYDDABER
Managing body   NCC.
Access   SH 6672. Car-park at Bont Newydd SE of Aber.
Habitat   Valley woodland, river.
Birds   Dipper, grey wagtail, buzzard, raven, woodland species.
Other information   Permit off rights of way. Nature trail.

COEDYDD MAENTWROG
Managing body   North Wales Naturalists' Trust/NT/NCC.
Access   SH 6742. Either through gate 50 yards from Oakeley Park Hotel on B4410 Rhyd – Maentwrog road, or along minor road along north side of Vale of Bronturnor and Doly-y-Moch SH 6641, or from Tan-y-Bwlch station on Ffestiniog railway, or from small car-park off B4410 Llyn Mair.
Habitat   Oak woodland, lake.
Birds   Buzzard, nuthatch, pied flycatcher, redstart, wood warbler, goldeneye, pochard.

CWM IDWALL
Managing body   NCC.
Access   SH 6459 and SH 6560. Footpath from A5 at Ogwen Cottage Mountain School.
Habitat   Mountain, lake, river.

Birds Herons, gulls, cormorant, dipper, common sandpiper, goldeneye, pochard, whooper swan, raven, ring ouzel.
Other information No entry to experimental enclosures.

CWMLLWYD WOOD
Managing body West Glamorgan County Council.
Access SS 6195.
Habitat Grassland, mixed woods, marsh, bog.
Birds Woodland species, winter snipe and woodcock.
Other information Two hides.

DOWROG COMMON
Managing body West Wales Naturalists' Trust.
Access SR 7727. Two miles NE of St Davids. Minor road crosses the common from A487 St Davids – Fishguard road. Tracks across road.
Habitat Lowland wet heath, willow carr, marsh, river, old clay pits.
Birds Wintering hen harrier, short-eared owl, merlin, whooper and Bewick's swans, wildfowl. Nesting moorhen, water rail, grasshopper and sedge warblers. Buzzard, kestrel, sparrowhawk.

DYFI
Managing body NCC.
Access SN 6194. Public footpath off A493 east of Aberdyfi and B4353 (south of river) minor road from B4353 at Ynyslas to dunes and parking area.
Habitat Estuary, dune system, raised bog, creeks, salt marsh, mud-flats.
Birds Wintering white-fronted goose, wigeon, teal, ringed plover, dunlin, sanderling, many other waders.
Other information Nature trail and information centre at Ynyslas Dunes. Permit required for bog.

GOODWICK MOOR
Managing body West Wales Naturalists' Trust.
Access SM 9438.
Habitat Reed-beds, marsh, bog, open water.
Birds Reed, grasshopper and sedge warblers, teal and snipe in winter.
Other information Permit away from footpaths.

KENFIG POOL AND DUNES
Managing body Mid-Glamorgan County Council.
Access SS 8081. Leave M4 at Junction 37. Reserve is ½ mile to west. From car-park at Kenfig on unclassified road between North Cornelly and Porthcawl.
Habitat Dunes, pool, reed-swamps, dune slacks.
Birds Winter – whooper and Bewick's swans, goldeneye, short-eared owl, merlin. Autumn – black tern, waders, sedge and grasshopper warblers, passage birds.
Other information Interpretive centre. Wellingtons advised.

NANT MELIN
Managing body West Wales Naturalists' Trust.
Access SN 7341. Cilycwm, 8 miles north of Llandovery and 6 miles NE from A428 road at Pumpsaint. Access by minor road from Rhandirmwynt to Cyrt-y-Cadno, leaving track by Bwlch-y-Rhiw and on to Brynaran Duon Farm.

Habitat   Mixed broad-leaved woods and valley.
Birds   Buzzard, raven, redstart, pied flycatcher, wood warbler, tree pipit.
Other information   Permit required.

NEWBOROUGH WARREN – YNYS LLANNDDWYN
Managing body   NCC.
Access   SH 4167/4363. A4080 South of Malltraeth.
Habitat   Sand-dunes, estuaries, salt marshes, dune grassland.
Birds   Curlew, lapwing, oystercatcher, meadow pipit, wintering duck, wildfowl – pintail, Canada and greylag geese, goldeneye, Bewick's and whooper swans, godwits, redshank, greenshank.
Other information   Permit off rights of way.

PEMBROKE UPPER MILL POND
Managing body   West Wales Naturalists' Trust.
Access   SM 9516.
Habitat   Open water.
Birds   Nesting little grebe. Visiting green sandpiper. Winter wildfowl, tufted duck, pochard, teal.

SOUTH GOWER COAST
Managing body   Glamorgan Naturalists' Trust and others.
Access   SS 4785 – Port Eynon, from car-park. SS 3585 – Overton via track at far end of village.
Habitat   Cliffs, shores, dunes, marshes.
Birds   Raven, kestrel, guillimot, fulmar, kittiwake, migrants, common scoter, reed and sedge warblers, bearded tit.

TAF FECHAN
Managing body   Merthyr Borough Council/Merthyr Naturalists' Society.
Access   SO 0410. Take A470 from Brecon to Merthyr Tydfil. Access beneath road bridge on entering Cefn-Coed-y-Cymmer one mile NW of Merthyr.
Habitat   Wooded river valley
Birds   Buzzard, dipper, grey wagtail, nuthatch, tree-creeper, raven, kingfisher, great spotted woodpecker, pied flycatcher, redstart, willow and wood warblers.

TEIFI VALLEY AND FORESHORE
Managing body   West Wales Naturalists' Trust.
Access   SN 1846.
Habitat   Mud-flats, river, shore.
Birds   Migrant and winter wildfowl, snipe, woodcock, teal, goldeneye, godwits, pintail.

TRAETH LAFAN
Managing body   Gwynedd County Council.
Access   SH 6172. Main road access along minor road from A55 near Tal-y-Bont (SH 6171) to coast beyond Aber Ogwen Farm.
Habitat   Intertidal sands, mud-flats, inland sands, freshwater steams.
Birds   Third most important site in Wales for wintering wildfowl – up to 14,000 of 10 species. Moulting great crested grebe and red-breasted merganser, breeding shelduck, terns, passage waders, wintering goldeneye and greenshank.

WHITEFORD BURROWS
Managing body   NCC.
Access   SS 4593. From Swansea take A483, turn left onto A4216 then right onto B4295 to Llanrhidian, continue west on minor road to Cheriton Park.
Habitat   Sand-dunes, salt marsh, foreshore.
Birds   Passage terns, whimbrel, waders. Winter – divers, grebes, brent goose, wigeon, pintail, shoveler, eider, hen harrier, grey plover, turnstone, sanderling, black-tailed godwit. All year – shelduck, oystercatcher, redshank, turnstone.
Other information   Permit off marked paths.

Northern England

ALLERTHORPE COMMON
Managing body   Yorkshire Wildlife Trust.
Access   SE 7747. Eastern access by track from Allerthorpe just south of A1079 York – Hull road, 7 miles west of Market Weighton. SE 7547. Western access – turn right 10 miles east of York on A1079 and follow signs to Thornton. Access path 1½ miles from A1079 is near bend in road.
Habitat   Wet heath, pools.
Birds   Curlew, nightjar, whinchat, snipe, woodcock.

ARNOLD
Managing body   Northumberland Wildlife Trust.
Access   NU 2520. Leave Alnwick on B1340, in 3 miles turn right on minor road to Craster. Public car-park in disused quarry.
Habitat   Scrub, woodland, stream, quarry.
Birds   Migrant passerines. Moulting site of lesser redpoll.

BEMPTON CLIFFS
Managing body   RSPB.
Access   TA 2074. Via cliff road from B1220 Flamborough – Filey road in Bempton village. Reserve is signposted.
Habitat   High chalk cliffs, topped with clay and small patches of scrub.
Birds   Sea-birds – kittiwake, razorbill, puffin, fulmar, herring gull, shag, only mainland colony of gannets. Passage skua, terns, waders and shearwater. Visitors include bluethroat, wheatear, ring ouzel, merlin, sparrow-hawk.
Other information   Very dangerous cliffs.

BIG WATERS
Managing body   Northumberland Wildlife Trust.
Access   NZ 2373. From A6107 turn onto B1318 (to Wide Open) 4 miles north of Newcastle. In 1 mile turn west at Traveller's Rest. Pass under by-pass and through Brunswick village. Turn north beyond Ca'Canny, along untarred road through gate to car-park. Walk through another gate and reserve is western part of lake.
Habitat   Lake, reed-beds, old ridge and furrow.
Birds   Nesting great crested grebe, wintering ducks, snipe. Large autumn swallow roost.
Other information   Hide (key from Trust office).

COCKLAWBURN DUNES
Managing body   Northumberland Wildlife Trust.
Access   NU 0149. East of Scremeston off A1 4 miles south of Berwick.
Habitat   Dunes, rocky shore, grassland.
Birds   Winter turnstone, purple sandpiper, divers, waders, sea-birds.

DENABY INGS
Managing body   Yorkshire Wildlife Trust.
Access   SE 5000. A6023 from Mexborough to Conisborough; fork left before canal at west end of Mexborough; follow High Melton road for 1 mile. Car-park and field station on right.
Habitat   Marsh, pools.
Birds   Great crested and little grebes, mallard, pochard, tufted duck, shoveler, snipe, reed and sedge warblers, passage and wintering birds.
Other information   Four hides – one suitable for wheelchairs.

FAIRBURN INGS
Managing body   RSPB.
Access   SE 4527. West side of A1 north of Ferrybridge at the village of Fairburn (signposted).
Habitat   Shallow lakes, marshes, flood pools, wooded spoil heaps, farmland.
Birds   Wintering wildfowl – teal, shoveler, pochard, tufted duck, goldeneye, goosander, coot, whooper swan. On passage – Arctic and black terns, little gulls, waders. Yellow and pied wagtails, sand martin. Nesting lapwing, redshank, snipe, little ringed plover, great crested and little grebes.
Other information   Wellingtons advised.

GRINDON LOUGH
Managing body   Northumberland Wildlife Trust.
Access   NY 8267. Turn north off A69 at Haydon Bridge to Grindon. In 3 miles turn left to Morwood. Park on roadside after 1 mile. No access allowed, view from road.
Habitat   Lake with rushes and sedges.
Birds   Breeding redshank, snipe, coot, yellow wagtail, little grebe. Winter wildfowl – bean, greylag, and pink-footed geese, whooper swan, golden plover.

HARBOTTLE CRAGS
Managing body   Northumberland Naturalists' Trust.
Access   NT 9204. From A697 Newcastle – Wooler road turn west onto B6344 to Rothbury. Continue west; leave B6341 3 miles west of Rothbury at Flotterton onto Alwinton road. Reserve is ½ mile west of Harbottle village. Park in Forestry Commission car-park.
Habitat   Crags, wetland, upland heather moor, lake.
Birds   Red and black grouse, ring ouzel, meadow pipit, wheatear, whinchat, curlew, lapwing, redshank, snipe, short-eared owl, kestrel, merlin.

HASKAYNE CUTTING
Managing body   Lancashire Trust for Nature Conservation/North West Water Authority.
Access   SD 3609. A567 west of Ormskirk, entrance by Barton Bridge on

Station Road, ¼ mile west of Blue Bell Inn.
Habitat   Disused railway cutting, grassland, marsh, scrub.
Birds   Warblers and other passerines.
Other information   Leaflet required as permit from Mrs B. Yorke, 3 Wicks Lane, Formby, Merseyside (070 48 72187).

HEALEY DELL
Managing body   Rochdale Borough Council.
Access   SD 8816.
Habitat   Moorland, river, wooded valley, marsh.
Birds   Woodland species – blackcap, garden warbler, woodcock, tawny owl, kestrel, snipe, redpoll, twite, pied and grey wagtails, siskin, waxwing.

HORNSEA MERE
Managing body   RSPB.
Access   TA 1947. From B1242 in Hornsea.
Habitat   Freshwater lake, reed-bed, mixed woodland, farmland.
Birds   Breeding reed warblers, wintering wildfowl – goldeneye, coot, mallard, teal, wigeon, tufted duck, gulls, waders, wheatear, whinchat, great crested grebe, reed and corn buntings, yellow wagtail.

LANCELOT CLARK STORTH
Managing body   Cumbria Trust for Nature Conservation.
Access   SD 5578. About 1 mile SE of Clawthorpe, 1½ miles east of M6 and 1½ miles NE of Burton. Further details from Trust.
Habitat   Woodland, limestone pavement, rough pasture.
Birds   Wren, woodcock, goldcrest, curlew, warblers, tree-creeper, long-tailed tit.

LINDISFARNE
Managing body   NCC.
Access   NU 1043. Several roads east of A1. Holy Island via Causeway (impassable at high tide) from Beal.
Habitat   Dunes, salt marshes, mud-flats.
Birds   Only regular British wintering ground for pale-bellied brent goose. Passage/winter wildfowl – long-tailed duck, wigeon, eider, mallard, greylag goose, whooper swan. Waders. Rarities – pine grosbeak, Richard's pipit.

MERE SANDS WOOD
Managing body   Lancashire Trust for Nature Conservation.
Access   SD 4516. Approach from B5246 via main track or public footpath. No vehicular access.
Habitat   Deciduous and conifer woodland, heathland, marsh, open water.
Birds   Turtle dove, great crested and little grebes, gadwall, shelduck, little ringed plover, whooper swan, grey goose.
Other information   Permit only – 20 Cousins Lane, Rufford, Lancs.

MOOR HOUSE
Managing body   NCC.
Access   NY 7332.
Habitat   Blanket bog, sheep walk.
Birds   Curlew, lapwing, golden plover, snipe, common sandpiper, red grouse, ring ouzel, meadow pipit, wheatear, dipper.
Other information   Leaflet available. Permit off public paths.

POTTERIC CARR
Managing body   Yorkshire Wildlife Trust.
Access   SE 5901. A630 Doncaster – Rotherham road, turn left at lights 1 mile outside Doncaster down Carr Hill. Go for 2 miles, cross M18 link road roundabout. Car-park 100 yards on left.
Habitat   Wetland, woods, grassland.
Birds   Nesting garganey, shoveler, tufted duck, pochard, water rail; visiting bittern, marsh harrier, sandpipers, black tern.
Other information   Seven hides, one accessible wheelchairs.

RIBBLE MARSHES
Managing body   NCC.
Access   SD 3723. Marine drive at Southport, overlooks wader roost, also viewing of sea-birds, wildfowl. No parking along Marine Drive. Park opposite sand works.
Habitat   Mud-flats and salt marshes.
Birds   Waders, wildfowl.

SIDDICK POND
Managing body   Allerdale District Council/NCC/Cumbria Trust for Nature Conservation.
Access   NY 0030. One mile north of Workington adjacent to A596.
Habitat   Shallow pond and reed-beds.
Birds   Winter wildfowl, 35 nesting species. Occasional visitors – black-necked grebe, black-tailed godwit, black tern, ruff, osprey.
Other information   Access arrangements with Park Manager, Allerdale District Council, Solway House, Mossbay Road, Workington (0900 4351).

SPURN PENINSULA
Managing body   Yorkshire Wildlife Trust.
Access   TA 4215. Approached by A1033 Hull – Partrington road and B1445 to Easington, thence by unclassified roads to Kinsea and Spurn. Vehicular access controlled.
Habitat   Sand and shingle peninsula, salt marsh, mud-flat.
Birds   Passage curlew, turnstone, dunlin, knot, redshank, terns, skuas, pied and spotted flycatchers, redstart, whinchat, redwing.

WAYOH RESERVOIR
Managing body   Lancashire Trust for Nature Conservation/North West Water Authority.
Access   SD 7317. Five miles north of Bolton. Public footpaths with access paths from Edgworth, Entwistle and Chapeltown.
Habitat   Open water, scrub, woodland, grassland, marsh.
Birds   Winter wildfowl, autumn passage waders, 7 species breeding warblers.
Other information   Permits off rights of way.

WHELDRAKE INGS
Managing body   Yorkshire Wildlife Trust.
Access   SE 6944. Eight miles SE of York; approached from either Wheldrake or Thorganby, 3/4 miles east of A19. Between the two villages turn sharp right, after ½ mile take narrow road on left leading to Wheldrake Bridge.
Habitat   Flood meadows, pool.

Birds Breeding mallard, shoveler, snipe, redshank, curlew, sedge and grasshopper warblers, heron, kestrel, barn and short-eared owls. Winter refuge for wildfowl and Bewick's swan.
Other information 1 April – 30 June. Open to members only.

Scotland

BALGAVIES LOCH
Managing body Scottish Wildlife Trust.
Access NO 5351. Car-park on A932 5 miles east of Forfar.
Habitat Loch, fen, woodland.
Birds Wintering wildfowl, greylag geese, water rail, woodcock, snipe, whooper swan, ruddy duck visit.
Other information Access restricted.

BALLANTRAE
Managing body Scottish Wildlife Trust.
Access NX 0882.
Habitat Lagoons, shingle spit.
Birds Little, common and Arctic terns, ringed plover, red-breasted merganser, common sandpiper.
Other information Access restricted mid-May – mid August (when little terns breeding).

BEINN EIGHE
Managing body NCC.
Access NG 0061. From car-park at Loch Maree.
Habitat Mountain, remnant Caledonian pine forest, lochs, moorland.
Birds Siskin, crossbill, ptarmigan, golden eagle, merlin, willow tit, goldcrest, redpoll.
Other information Access restricted. Contact Warden: Kinlochewe 254 or 244, or Aultroy visitor centre: Kinlochewe 257.

BLACKWOOD OF RANNOCH
Managing body Forestry Commission.
Access NN 5755.
Habitat Pine forest.
Birds Capercaillie, black grouse, siskin, Scottish crossbill, redstart, spotted flycatcher, tree pipit.
Other information Access restricted to forest tracks starting at NN 5956 and 5450 (no car access to these points).

CAIRNGORMS
Managing body NCC.
Access Huge reserve with many access points.
Habitat Mountains, moorlands, forest, rivers.
Birds Crested tit, crossbill, siskin, redstart, tree pipit, willow warbler, capercaillie, red grouse, peregrine, ring ouzel, dotterel, ptarmigan, golden eagle, merlin, buzzard, sparrow-hawk.

CULBIN SANDS
Managing body   RSPB.
Access   NH 9058. East along shore from Nairn on the junction of the A96 and A939, 1 mile east of Nairn.
Habitat   Foreshore on Moray Firth, sand-flats, salt marsh, shingle bars, sand-dune system, woodland.
Birds   Wintering bar-tailed godwit, oystercatcher, dunlin, ringed plover, redshank, curlew, red-breasted merganser, greylag goose. Common and velvet scoters and long-tailed duck off shore. Little and common terns.
Other information   Open at all times along shore from Kintessack. Dangerous tides.

FOUNTAINBLEAU AND LADY PARK
Managing body   Scottish Wildlife Trust.
Access   NX 9977. On NE edge of Dumfries between A709 Dumfries – Lockerbie road and A701 (T) Dumfries – Moffat road. Access from Dumfries High School.
Habitat   Wet woodland.
Birds   Willow tit, redpoll, spotted flycatcher, warblers, reed bunting.
Other information   Permit from 25 Rotchell Park, Dumfries.

GLEN AFFRIC
Managing body   Forestry Commission.
Access   NH 2424.
Habitat   Native pinewood.
Birds   Scottish crossbill, capercaillie, black grouse, goosander, dipper, grey wagtail, raptors.

KEN-DEE MARSHES
Managing body   RSPB.
Access   NX 6476 (Kenmure Holms).
NX 6969 (River Dee Marshes).
Lies on western side of A714 New Galloway – Castle Douglas road.
Habitat   Alluvial meadows, freshwater marshes, hillside, farmland, woodland.
Birds   Wintering white-fronted and greylag geese, wigeon, pintail, mallard, shoveler, goosander, whooper swan, merlin, kestrel, sparrow-hawk, peregrine, buzzard, redshank, snipe, great crested grebe, grasshopper and willow warblers.
Other information   Good views from A713 on east and minor road and A762 on west. Escorted visits by arrangement with Warden: Midtown, Laurieston, Nr. Castle Douglas.

KILLIECRANKIE
Managing body   RSPB.
Access   NN 9163. West of A9 Pitlochry – Blair Atholl road.
Habitat   Sessile oakwoods, gorse, river, moorland, farmland.
Birds   Wood warbler, tree pipit, garden warbler, redstart, woodpeckers, crossbill, buzzard, kestrel, sparrow-hawk, black grouse, raven.
Other information   Escorted visiting April – August by arrangement with Warden: Balrobbie, Killiecrankie, Pitlochry, Perthshire.

LINDEAN RESERVOIR
Managing body Borders Regional Council.
Access NT 5128.
Habitat Reservoir with islands and woodland.
Birds Breeding and wintering duck, whinchat, sedge warbler, linnet.

LOCH FLEET
Managing body Scottish Wildlife Trust.
Access NH 7796.
Habitat Tidal basin, pinewood, shingle.
Birds Shelduck, redshank, oystercatcher, curlew, golden plover, knot, wintering duck, red-breasted merganser, common scoter, long-tailed duck, eider, capercaillie, siskin, crossbill.
Other information Access to woodland restricted. Permit from Sutherland Estates Office.

LOCH OF STRATHBEG
Managing body RSPB.
Access NK 0759. North of A952 Peterhead – Fraserburgh road near village of Crimond.
Habitat Shallow loch, sand-dunes, freshwater fen, marsh, salt marsh, woodland, farmland.
Birds Wintering whooper swan, ducks, greylag and pink-footed geese, red-breasted merganser, goosander, smew, mallard, wigeon, breeding eider, tufted duck, water rail, sedge warbler.
Other information Permit in advance (as access across MOD property) from The Lythe, Crimonmogate, Lonmau, Fraserburgh.

LOCHWINNOCH
Managing body RSPB.
Access NS 3558. Off A760 ½ mile east of Lochwinnoch.
Habitat Loch, meadow, sedge and reed marsh, deciduous woodland.
Birds Great crested grebe, little grebe, black-headed gull, mallard, shoveler, pochard, sedge and willow warblers, reed bunting, wintering greylag goose, whooper swan, wigeon, teal, goosander, waders, kestrel, sparrow-hawk.

LONGHAVEN CLIFFS
Managing body Scottish Wildlife Trust.
Access NK 1239.
Habitat Granite cliffs.
Birds About 23,000 pairs nesting sea-birds – herring gull, greater and lesser black-backed gulls, kittiwake, guillemot, shag, puffin.

MONTROSE BASIN
Managing body Scottish Wildlife Trust.
Access NO 6958. From A934 and A935 east of Montrose.
Habitat Estuarine tidal basin, sand and mud-flats.
Birds Nationally important for wintering waders and wildfowl – redshank, knot, wigeon, eider and over 5,000 pink-footed geese.
Other information Hide facilities by arrangement with Ranger: North Fillysole Cottage, Kinnaird Estate, by Brechin, Angus 035 62 3480.

MUIR OF DINNET
Managing body NCC.
Access NO 4399.
Habitat Moorland, woodland, bog, open water.
Birds Willow warbler, redpoll, woodcock, wildfowl, whooper swan, greylag and pink-footed geese, pintail, gadwall, shoveler, merlin, hen harrier, black grouse.

PASS OF AYVOAN
Managing body Scottish Wildlife Trust.
Access NH 9910. Glenmore – Nethy Bridge road passes through the reserve. Access from car-park at Glenmore Forest Centre by walking along the Forestry Commission track past Glenmore Lodge.
Habitat Remnant of old Glenmore Caledonian Forest. Scree slopes.
Birds Crossbill, goldcrest, crested tit, tree pipit, redstart, grey wagtail.

ST CYRUS
Managing body NCC.
Access NO 7463.
Habitat Foreshore, dunes, cliffs.
Birds Little tern, grasshopper warbler, stonechat, whitethroat, yellow-hammer, fulmar, migrants, passage skua and shearwater, winter divers and waders.
Other information Access restricted in tern breeding season, May – August. Leaflet and comprehensive report from NCC.

SEATON CLIFFS
Managing body Scottish Wildlife Trust.
Access NO 6742. Parking at north end of promenade at Arbroath. Along cliff to footpath through reserve.
Habitat Red sandstone cliffs.
Birds Fulmar, kittiwake, guillimot, eider, migrants.

SANDS OF FORVIE AND YTHAN ESTUARY
Managing body NCC.
Access NK 0227. From car-parks on A975 north of Newburgh.
Habitat Foreshore, sand-dunes, cliffs, moorland, estuary.
Birds Largest breeding colony of eiders in UK, kittiwake, fulmar, 4 species of terns, grey goose, waders on estuary in autumn and winter.
Other information Permit only away from paths and foreshore. Hide overlooking ternery. Leaflet and handbook from NCC.

THREAVE WILDFOWL REFUGE
Managing body National Trust for Scotland.
Access NX 7462.
Habitat Rivers, islands, marshes.
Birds Wildfowl including greylag goose, wigeon, teal.

YETHOLM LOCH
Managing body Scottish Wildlife Trust.
Access NT 8028. Off B6352, turning to Lochtower (unmetalled road).
Habitat Loch and marshland.
Birds Breeding great crested grebe, shoveler, teal, pochard, wintering whooper swan, pink-footed goose, ducks.

Useful Addresses

British Birds Magazine
Fountains, Blunham, Bedford, MK44 3NJ

British Trust for Ornithology
Beech Grove, Tring, Hertfordshire, HP23 5NR

International Council for Bird Preservation
219c Huntingdon Road, Cambridge, CB3 0DL

National Trust
42 Queen Anne's Gate, London, SW1

Nature Conservancy Council
19 Belgrave Square, London, SW1

Royal Society for Nature Conservation
The Green, Nettleham, Lincolnshire, LN2 2NR

(Contact above for addresses of local Naturalists' Trusts and Trusts
for Nature Conservation.)

Royal Society for the Protection of Birds
The Lodge, Sandy, Bedfordshire, SG19 2DL

Society for the Promotion of Nature Reserves
The Manor House, Alford, Lincolnshire

Wildfowl Trust
Slimbridge, Gloucestershire, GL2 7BT

Woodland Trust
Westgate, Grantham, Lincolnshire, NG31 6LL